QUICHES AND FLANS

A selection of versatile and mouth-watering recipes using a wide range of pastries and wholesome fillings – with hints on economic and easy preparation.

D1428246

By the same author

A VEGETARIAN IN THE FAMILY
THE RAW FOOD WAY TO HEALTH
THE WHOLEFOOD LUNCH BOX
THE WHOLEFOOD SWEETS BOOK
PIZZAS AND PANCAKES
PASTA DISHES
SIMPLE AND SPEEDY WHOLEFOOD COOKING

QUICHES AND FLANS

by

JANET HUNT

Illustrated by Clive Birch

THORSONS PUBLISHERS LIMITED
Wellingborough, Northamptonshire

First published May 1982
Second Impression October 1982

© JANET HUNT 1982

This book is sold subject to the condition that it shall not, by way of trade or otherwise, be lent, re-sold, hired out, or otherwise circulated without the publisher's prior consent in any form of binding or cover other than that in which it is published and without a similar condition including this condition being imposed on the subsequent purchaser.

British Library Cataloguing in Publication Data

Hunt, Janet
    Quiches and flans.
    1. Vegetarian cookery 2. Quiches (Cookery)
    3. Pancakes, waffles, etc.
    I. Title
    641.5'636   TX837

    ISBN 0-7225-0722-4

Typeset by Glebe Graphics, Wilby, Northamptonshire.
Printed and bound in Great Britain by
Richard Clay (The Chaucer Press) Ltd.,
Bungay, Suffolk.

CONTENTS

Wholefoods, quite simply, are foods in their natural state – nothing added, nothing taken away. In this age of mass-production foods, wholefoods are not always easy to obtain. But as nutritionalists and doctors become increasingly convinced, of their value in building and maintaining health, so their availability is fast improving.

Include as many natural, unadulterated foods as you can in your day to day eating pattern, and discover not just exciting new tastes and a fresh approach to mealtimes, but better health too.

BEFORE YOU BEGIN

There is nothing new about the idea of cooking a mixture of selected ingredients together in their own edible shell or 'wrapping'. Indian samosas, Chinese egg rolls, Italian ravioli, American blueberry pie, English pasties – all are based on the same principle. Another thing they have in common is their undoubted popularity, both in their own countries and abroad. Open-topped flans are yet a further variation on this same theme, one that offers visual pleasure as well as tasting and smelling mouth-wateringly good.

For the cook, flans can be a culinary challenge – or just a surprisingly quick and relatively easy way to feed a hungry family. When time is short, a flan can be thrown together from the simplest ingredients, even left-overs, and if the shell is made from crumbs instead of pastry the whole dish can be on the table in less than half an hour. Or if you wish, you can spend hours preparing a flan that will deserve its place (and praise) as the centre-piece at a very special meal.

Because they are so versatile, flans can also be as wholesome as you choose to make them. Look through the following recipes and you will get the idea. Quiches, which are based on the original quiche recipe from Lorraine, France, contain a savoury custard, traditionally made from eggs, cream and cheese; so if you prefer not to use dairy produce, try the flans instead. And do not forget that sweet flans make an unusual dessert at the end of a light meal, as well as a tasty and nutritious substitute for cake, at any time.

FLAN-MAKING TIPS

Use 100 per cent wholemeal flour whenever possible. If you find it difficult to handle at first, you can sieve out the bran to make it finer, or use 81 per cent wholemeal flour (which has more of the fibre removed), or a combination of 100 per cent and 81 per cent.

Because wholemeal flour is less glutinous than white, it makes a more crumbly dough. There are a number of things you can do to help overcome this. Ingredients, utensils, the temperature of the room (*and* your hands) should be as cool as possible. If you can leave the prepared dough in the fridge or somewhere cool for at least half an hour before rolling it out, so much the better. Check that your dough is moist enough – the bran in the flour will soak up a lot of liquid, and as the amount of bran varies, it is hard to give exact amounts of water needed. If the dough is dry and crumbly, add a spoonful or two of water as you go along.

Rolling your pastry between two sheets of aluminium or cling foil helps prevent crumbling. It helps in another way too. Pick up the rolled out pastry still in the wrapping, remove one sheet, lay the pastry in the flan dish and peel off the other sheet. This way your pastry is easier to handle; less likely to come apart whilst you manoeuvre it into position.

Make sure your pastry is rolled our slightly larger than needed – if you stretch it, it will probably shrink again during cooking. Press it firmly against the flan dish as trapped air will expand in the heat of the oven, and may push the pastry up through the filling. A pre-heated oven also helps ensure good results.

The simplest way to bake pastry 'blind' is to roll it out and line your flan dish, prick the dough and cover with aluminium foil, then bake for 10 minutes or so at the recommended temperature. Another way is to line the dish with pastry, cover with foil or greaseproof paper, and fill with beans or rice (kept specially for the task!), but this seems unnecessarily complicated.

Many cooks, when making flans or quiches, prefer to bake their pastry blind every time. Although it gives a crisper pastry, it does add an extra step to an already lengthy procedure, so in most of the following recipes, it is only recommended when the filling is especially soft and liquid. You can, of course, bake your pastry blind for any recipe.

Choice of *kind* of pastry is also up to you. Traditionally, plain shortcrust pastry is used with most savoury and sweet flans as the richer fillings are best off-set by a plain base. If cookery is to you a creative art, a chance to experiment and *not* just follow rules, you may want to try some of the other pastries given here. All of them are full of goodness, and if they change the taste and texture of your finished flan, you may well have some very pleasant surprises. When making sweet flans in a pastry base, there is no need to add sugar to the dough, especially if the filling is extra sweet. If, however, you prefer sweet pastry, add one or two tablespoonsful of raw cane sugar to the flour before mixing with other ingredients.

Quantities given match up generally with those given in the recipes, though you may find you have some dough left over. In this case, either use it to make a decorative lattice top, or keep it in the freezer to use on another occasion.

A selection of cases made with biscuits, cereals and crispbreads is also included for those who have less time, or less patience! When using any of them, you will find it much easier to remove the flan from the tin if you first grease it very lightly, then line it with silver foil. Press this firmly against the edges, leaving an overlap that can be pressed down against the *outside* edge, and used as a grip in order to lift the cooked flan out of the tin. Then simply peel off the silver foil and discard.

A brief word about ingredients. Based on the assumption that food should do you good as well as taste good, the recipes are based on wholefood ingredients, i.e. those that are as near to their natural state as possible, with nothing removed, nothing added. Most of them are now available not only at health food and wholefood shops, but from supermarkets too.

What you will *not* find included here (except on the very rare occasions when there is no 'natural' alternative), are refined foods such as white flour, sugar, rice; lifeless foods like dried vegetables, artificial flavourings; dubious foods including meat, now produced in such a way that it contains almost as many additives as it does nutrients.

Flours are wholemeal, preferably 100 per cent. Soft margarine should be low in cholesterol, high in polyunsaturates (read the label), or a harder version can be used providing it is made with vegetable oils. Sugars should be raw – if you cannot get the exact kind specified, try using the one you *can* get, or use honey, pure maple syrup or molasses. Nuts and seeds should be uncooked, unsalted.

Dairy products feature largely in many of these dishes, but even so they should be used as sparingly as possible if you are at all concerned about cholesterol. Feel free to adapt – for example, yogurt is healthier than cream, but cream can make a delicious difference in some recipes, so why not combine them? Or use mostly single cream with just a spoonful or two of double to thicken it up? Cheeses, too, can be adjusted to suit your tastes and requirements. Edam is lower in fat than Cheddar. Curd, cottage or *Quark* cheese can replace cream cheese, or use half and half. Eggs, which should be free-range for the sake of your health *and* the chickens', can be reduced in number. Or you can add one or two whipped egg whites to a quiche or flan for more nutrition without boosting calories or cholesterol – you will also get a fluffier, lighter textured filling. Milk can be skimmed if you prefer (add an extra spoonful or two of powdered milk to make it creamier *and* richer in protein). Fresh goat's milk can replace cow's milk, and plant or soya milks and creams go well in the recipes too.

It goes without saying that fruit and vegetables should be fresh, although the frozen kind can be used in an emergency. Fresh herbs are infinitely better than the dried variety – once you get used to using them; why not grow your own? Other 'extras' that make such a big difference for such little cost are sea salt, freshly ground pepper and spices, natural essences. Be imaginative with your use of ingredients and garnishes, enjoy your time in the kitchen, and the results will be enjoyed by everyone lucky enough to be invited to sample your flans and quiches.

All recipes are for 4 people.

PASTRY RECIPES

BASIC SHORTCRUST PASTRY

8 oz (225g) plain wholemeal flour (or half plain, half
   self-raising)
4 oz (100g) polyunsaturated margarine
Approx. 2 tablespoonsful cold water
Pinch of sea salt

1. Sieve the flour into a bowl with the salt.

2. Use fingertips to rub the margarine into the flour to form a
   mixture resembling fine crumbs.

3. With a round-edged knife blend in the water gradually, then
   knead a little – the dough should be soft, yet firm enough to
   gather into a ball.

4. Wrap in aluminium or cling foil and chill in fridge for at least
   half an hour, if possible.

5. Roll out and use as required.

Note: This quantity of pastry will line a 7-8 in. flan dish.

ALL-IN-ONE SHORTCRUST PASTRY

8 oz (225 g) plain wholemeal flour
5 oz (150 g) polyunsaturated margarine (straight from fridge)
Approx. 2 tablespoonsful cold water
Pinch of sea salt

1. Sieve the flour, add the salt.

2. Using a fork, mix together the margarine, water, and half of the flour.

3. Gradually stir in the rest of the flour so that a firm dough is formed, then turn onto a lightly floured board and knead thoroughly until dough is silky smooth in texture.

4. Wrap in aluminium or cling foil and chill in fridge for at least half an hour, if possible.

5. Roll out and use as required.

Note: This quantity of pastry will line a 7-8 in. flan dish.

SHORTCRUST PASTRY WITH EGG

6 oz (175 g) plain wholemeal flour
3 oz (75 g) polyunsaturated margarine
1 tablespoonful cold water
1 medium-sized egg
Pinch of sea salt

1. Sieve the flour into a bowl with the salt.

2. Rub in the fat to form a mixture like fine crumbs.

3. With a round-edged knife stir the beaten egg into the mixture, then add the water to form a dough.

4. Knead the dough for a few minutes, adding more flour if it is sticky, a little water if it is too dry.

5. Roll out and use as required.

Note: This quantity of pastry will line a 7-8 in. flan dish.

WHEAT AND SOYA PASTRY

6 oz (175 g) plain wholemeal flour
2 oz (50 g) soya flour
3 tablespoonsful vegetable oil
Cold water to mix
Pinch of sea salt

1. Sieve together the soya flour, wholemeal flour and salt.

2. Using a fork, blend in the oil.

3. Add enough water to make a firm but pliable dough.

4. Wrap in aluminium or cling foil and chill in fridge.

5. Roll out and use as required.

Note: This quantity of pastry will line an 8-9 in. flan dish.

BASIC VEGAN PASTRY

8 oz (225 g) plain wholemeal flour
1 teaspoonful baking powder
3 tablespoonsful vegetable oil
3 tablespoonsful cold water
Pinch of sea salt

1.   Combine the flour, baking-powder and salt.

2.   Combine the oil and water.

3.   Stir the liquid into the flour, and mix thoroughly, but as rapidly as possible.

4.   Wrap in aluminium or cling foil and chill in fridge for at least half an hour.

5.   Roll out and use as required.

Note: This quantity of pastry will line a 7-8 in. flan dish.

FLAKY PASTRY

8 oz (225 g) plain wholemeal flour
2 teaspoonsful baking powder
6 oz (175 g) polyunsaturated margarine
Barely ¼ pt (150 ml) cold water
Pinch of sea salt

1. Sift the flour with the baking powder and salt.

2. Divide the margarine into three portions and rub one of them into the flour, then add enough water to make a soft dough.

3. On a floured board roll the dough to an oblong shape.

4. Flake another portion of the margarine onto two thirds of the dough, leaving the last third without fat.

5. Fold the bottom of the pastry up, and the top down to make an 'envelope' of the dough, then seal the open edges by pressing with a rolling pin.

6. Re-roll, then use the last portion of margarine in the same way.

7. Roll out the pastry again, and if it is still firm to handle, repeat rolling and folding once more. (If it is sticky, leave it in the fridge for a while before the final rolling out.)

8. Return to fridge again as cold pastry is easier to handle, and will also rise better.

9. Roll out and use as required.

Note: This quantity of pastry will line a large flan dish. As the process is complicated, it is a good idea to make this amount at a time, and to freeze any extra until needed.

ALL-IN-ONE FLAKY PASTRY

8 oz (225 g) plain wholemeal flour
1/3 pt (200 ml) boiling water
3 tablespoonsful vegetable oil
Pinch of sea salt

1. Add the oil to the boiling water.

2. Using a whisk or blender, beat the water and oil together vigorously until thoroughly blended.

3. Beat in the combined flour and salt to make a firm dough.

4. Knead briefly, then wrap in aluminium or cling foil and chill in fridge for at least half an hour.

5. Roll out and use as required.

Note: This quantity of pastry will line a 7-8 in. flan dish.

SWEET FLEUR PASTRY

4 oz (100g) plain wholemeal flour
2½ oz (65g) polyunsaturated margarine
1 egg yolk
1 oz (25g) raw cane sugar
Cold water to mix

1. Cream together the margarine and sugar.

2. Sprinkle in the flour and use a wooden spoon to mix well.

3. Add the lightly beaten egg yolk, and enough water to make a firm dough.

4. Roll out and use as required.

Note: This quantity of pastry will line a 6-7 in. flan dish.

SAVOURY FILLINGS

CASHEW NUT FLAN

Pastry to line an 8 in. flan dish
4 oz (100 g) ground cashew nuts
1 medium onion
1 oz (25 g) polyunsaturated margarine
¼ pt (150 ml) milk
1 large egg
1 teaspoonful marjoram
Parsley
Seasoning to taste

1. Prepare and roll out pastry; use it to line a flan dish.

2. Melt the margarine in a pan, and *sauté* the finely chopped onion for a minute or two.

3. Add the ground cashews, milk, marjoram and seasoning, and mix well.

4. Remove from heat and cool slightly before adding the well beaten egg.

5. Pour mixture into the flan case, smooth the top, and bake at 350°F/180°C (Gas Mark 4) for 35-40 minutes. Garnish with chopped parsley and serve hot.

SORREL AND SESAME QUICHE

For Pastry
Pastry to line an 8 in. flan dish
2 oz (50g) sesame seeds, raw or roasted

For Filling
Approx. 1 lb (450g) fresh sorrel
6 oz (175g) cream cheese
2 eggs
Pinch of nutmeg
Seasoning to taste

1. Mix the sesame seeds into the dough before rolling it out and lining a flan dish.

2. Bake the pastry blind for 10 minutes at 400°F/205°C (Gas Mark 6).

3. Meanwhile, carefully wash the sorrel, then steam it for 5 minutes, or until tender. Gently press out the excess water, then chop the sorrel finely.

4. Put it into a bowl with the cream cheese, seasoning and nutmeg, and blend well until the cheese melts to form a creamy sauce. Cool slightly, then beat in the eggs.

5. Spoon the sorrel into the prepared flan case; spread it evenly; bake at 350°F/180°C (Gas Mark 4) for about 30 minutes. Serve hot or cold.

Note: Wild sorrel tastes something like spinach, but is, at the same time, deliciously different. If you cannot find it, use spinach instead.

ASPARAGUS AND EGG FLAN

Pastry to line an 8 in. flan dish
10 oz (275 g) fresh or frozen asparagus
1 oz (25 g) polyunsaturated margarine
1 oz (25 g) plain wholemeal flour
½ pt (275 ml) milk
4 eggs
1 oz (25 g) wholemeal breadcrumbs
1 oz (25 g) Cheddar cheese
1 teaspoonful tarragon
Seasoning to taste

1. Roll out the pastry and line the flan dish.

2. If using frozen asparagus, cook according to instructions. Fresh asparagus should be washed and trimmed, then tied in bundles and steamed in a tall pan for about 20 minutes, or until the shoots are tender.

3. Arrange the drained asparagus in the flan case.

4. Hard boil the eggs, cool slightly, then cut in slices and lay them evenly on top of the asparagus.

5. Melt the margarine, add the flour and cook briefly, then take the pan off the heat and pour in the milk.

6. Continue cooking and stirring until the sauce thickens, then add tarragon and seasoning. Wait a few minutes before pouring the sauce into the flan case.

7. Finally, top with breadcrumbs and grated cheese.

8. Bake the flan at 375°F/190°C (Gas Mark 5) for about 30 minutes.

CELERIAC FLAN AU GRATIN

Pastry to line an 8 in. flan dish
1 large or 2 small celeriacs
1 oz (25 g) polyunsaturated margarine or vegetable oil
1 oz (25 g) plain wholemeal flour
½ pt (275 ml) milk
4 oz (100 g) grated Cheddar cheese
Seasoning to taste

1. Roll out pastry and use to line a flan dish.

2. Top, tail and peel the celeriac, then cut into cubes and steam or cook in minimum amount of water for about 30 minutes, or until tender but still crisp.

3. Meanwhile heat the margarine in a pan and gently *sauté* the flour for a few minutes.

4. Remove from the heat and stir in the milk; return to the heat and bring to boil, still stirring, until sauce thickens.

5. Add most of the cheese and seasoning.

6. Strain the celeriac and mix with the cheese sauce, then leave to cool a few minutes before putting the mixture into the flan case.

7. Sprinkle the rest of the grated cheese over the top, and bake at 400°F/205°C (Gas Mark 6) for 30 minutes.

Note: Similar to celery in taste, this turnip shaped root vegetable is delicious served in this way. If you cannot find celeriac at your greengrocers, use celery instead.

ASPARAGUS QUICHE WITH YOGURT

For Base
4 oz (100 g) wholemeal breadcrumbs
Small carton plain yogurt
Seasoning to taste

For Filling
8 oz (225 g) fresh or frozen asparagus tips
3 eggs
¼ pt (150 ml) milk
Small carton plain yogurt
4 oz (100 g) Gruyère or Cheddar cheese
Fresh parsley
Seasoning to taste

1. Combine the bread crumbs with the yogurt and seasoning, tip into an 8 in. flan dish, and press the mixture down to form an even lining on the base and sides.

2. Lightly steam the asparagus if fresh; cook according to instructions if frozen. Drain well.

3. Beat the eggs, add the milk, yogurt, seasoning and parsley.

4. Arrange most of the asparagus in the flan case, keeping a few pieces for decoration.

5. Spread the grated cheese over the asparagus, then pour in the egg mixture and top with the reserved asparagus tips.

6. Bake at 375°F/190°C (Gas Mark 5) for 30-35 minutes, or until set. Serve hot or warm.

HERBED CABBAGE FLAN

For Base
6 oz (175g) plain wholemeal flour
3 oz (75g) polyunsaturated margarine
Seasoning to taste

For Filling
1 small white cabbage
2 medium onions
1 tablespoonful vegetable oil
4 oz (100g) curd cheese
1 teaspoonful basil
1 teaspoonful rosemary
2 teaspoonsful parsley
1 oz (25g) sunflower seeds, raw or roasted
1 oz (25g) polyunsaturated margarine
Seasoning to taste

1. Use fingertips to rub the margarine into the flour to make a crumb-like mixture; season, then press into a lightly greased flan dish.

2. Bake at 400°F/205°C (Gas Mark 6) for 15 minutes.

3. Meanwhile, shred and lightly steam the cabbage until tender but still crisp. Drain.

4. Heat the oil and *sauté* the sliced onions for a few minutes, then drain and combine with the cabbage.

5. Add the curd cheese, stirring well until it melts to make a creamy sauce, then sprinkle in the herbs and seasoning.

6. Pile mixture into the flan case, sprinkle with seeds, dot with the remaining margarine, and continue baking for 10-15 minutes.

LEEK FLAN WITH POTATO PASTRY

For Base
4 oz (100g) potatoes
5 oz (150g) plain wholemeal flour
3 oz (75g) polyunsaturated margarine
1 teaspoonful baking powder

For Filling
1 lb (450g) leeks
3 medium tomatoes
4 oz (100g) cream or curd cheese
2 oz (50g) Cheddar cheese
1 teaspoonful mixed herbs
Seasoning to taste

1. Peel the potatoes, cut into cubes, and steam until soft enough to mash.

2. Sieve together the flour and baking powder.

3. Mix the potato *purée* with the flour, then add the creamed margarine, blending all the ingredients thoroughly.

4. On a lightly floured board knead the potato dough for a few minutes, then roll out, and use to line an 8 in. flan dish.

5. Clean, trim, and cut the leeks into 1 in. segments, then steam until just tender. Drain and cool slightly.

6. Stir in the cream cheese until it melts to make a thick sauce. Season.

7. Spoon the mixture into the flan case, arrange the sliced tomatoes on top; then sprinkle with grated cheese and herbs mixed together.

8. Bake at 350°F/180°C (Gas Mark 4) for 30 minutes, or until flan case is cooked. Serve hot.

SOYA CREAMED PEA AND MUSHROOM FLAN

Pastry to line an 8 in. flan dish
8 oz (225 g) peas, fresh or frozen
4 oz (100 g) mushrooms
2 tablespoonsful vegetable oil
1 oz (25 g) soya flour
1 oz (25 g) plain wholemeal flour
½ pt (275 ml) soya milk (home-made, tinned or made up
  from soya powder)
Parsley
A little fine oatmeal – if necessary
Seasoning to taste

1. Line the flan dish with the prepared and rolled out pastry;
    bake blind at 400°F/205°C (Gas Mark 6) for 10 minutes.

2. Cook the peas until just tender, then drain well.

3. Heat half the oil and gently *sauté* the washed, sliced mush-
    rooms for 5 minutes, turning frequently. Drain on a paper
    towel and set aside.

4. Mix together the flour and soya flour in a bowl.

5. Heat the rest of the oil and add the flours; *sauté* for a minute
    or two, then gently pour in the soya milk.

6. Continue heating until mixture boils and sauce thickens,
    stirring all the time.

7. Add the mushrooms, peas and seasoning. If the sauce is too
    liquid, sprinkle the mixture with some fine oatmeal, stir it
    well in, and cook for a few minutes longer.

8. Spoon vegetables and sauce into the prepared flan case, and
    bake at 350°F/180°C (Gas Mark 4) for 20 minutes, or until
    pastry is cooked. Serve hot garnished with plenty of coarsely
    chopped parsley.

FENNEL QUICHE
(Italian Style)

Pastry to line an 8 in. flan dish
1 lb (450g) fennel bulbs
2 oz (50g) polyunsaturated margarine
6 oz (175g) mozzarella or bel paese cheese
3 eggs
2 oz (50g) grated Parmesan cheese
¼ pt (150ml) cream or creamy milk
Fresh parsley
Seasoning to taste

1. Roll out the pastry; line the flan dish; bake pastry blind at 400°F/205°C (Gas Mark 6) for 10 minutes.

2. Boil the fennel bulbs until just tender. Drain well, then cut into slices from top to bottom, and dry with a paper towel.

3. Heat the margarine and gently *sauté* the fennel slices, until they begin to brown. Turn and cook other side.

4. Layer fennel across base of flan, then top with slices of the mozzarella or bel paese cheese.

5. Beat together the eggs, grated cheese and cream, and season well. Pour into the flan case, and sprinkle with the chopped parsley.

6. Bake at 375°F/190°C (Gas Mark 5) for 30 minutes, or until the filling has set. Serve hot.

CAULIFLOWER FLAN 'SOUFFLÉ'

For Base
4 oz (100g) rolled oats
2 oz (50g) plain wholemeal flour
2 tablespoonsful vegetable oil
Water to mix
Pinch of sea salt

For Filling
1 medium cauliflower
4 oz (100g) Cheddar cheese
4 oz (100g) ground sunflower seeds
2 oz (50g) wheat germ
Pinch of nutmeg
Seasoning to taste

1. Combine the oatmeal and flour; stir in the oil.

2. Add cold water to make a firm dough; knead for a few minutes, then press as evenly as possible against the base and sides of an 8 in. flan dish.

3. Steam the cauliflower until tender.

4. Put the chopped cauliflower in a blender with enough of the water in which it was cooked to make a thick, smooth *purée*.

5. Grate the Cheddar cheese, and add it to the cauliflower with the ground seeds, wheat germ and seasoning.

6. Pour it into the flan case and top with nutmeg.

7. Bake at 375°F/190°C (Gas Mark 5) for 20-30 minutes, or until flan base is crisp, and *soufflé* filling is set. Serve hot.

CHEESE AND RICE FLAN

Pastry to line an 8 in. flan dish
1 large onion
1 tablespoonful vegetable oil
4 oz (100g) cooked brown rice
4 oz (100g) Cheddar cheese
1 large egg
2 teaspoonsful curry powder
3 large tomatoes
Pinch of garam masala
Seasoning to taste

1. Roll out the pastry and use to line a flan dish.

2. Fry the sliced onion in the heated oil until just beginning to brown; drain, and lay on base of flan.

3. In a bowl, mix together the rice, grated cheese, curry powder, seasoning and beaten egg.

4. Spoon the mixture into the flan case and top with slices of tomato and a good pinch of garam masala.

5. Bake at 350°F/180°C (Gas Mark 4) for about 40 minutes. Serve hot.

CRUNCHY COURGETTE FLAN

Pastry to line an 8 in. flan dish
1 oz (25 g) polyunsaturated margarine
3 medium courgettes
1 large onion
3 medium tomatoes
4 oz (100g) wholemeal breadcrumbs
4 oz (100g) chopped walnuts
2 oz (50g) Cheddar cheese
Good pinch of chilli powder
Good pinch of mixed herbs
Seasoning to taste

1. Line a flan dish with the pastry, and bake blind at 400°F/205°C (Gas Mark 6) for 10 minutes.

2. Meanwhile, wash the courgettes, then chop them into smallish pieces and *sauté*, together with the sliced onion, in the margarine.

3. Add the bread crumbs and continue cooking gently for a few minutes more. Chop and add the tomatoes.

4. Remove from heat and combine with the walnuts, chilli powder, herbs and seasoning.

5. Spoon into the flan case, smooth as well as you can, and scatter with the grated cheese.

6. Return flan to the oven for a further 15 minutes, or until pastry is crisp, and cheese topping melted.

BEAN SPROUT QUICHE

Pastry to line an 8 in. flan dish
4 oz (100g) fresh bean sprouts
2 eggs
½ pt (275 ml) milk
3 oz (75 g) Emmenthal cheese
Seasoning to taste

1. Line a flan dish with the prepared, rolled out pastry.

2. Cover the base with the bean sprouts, spread evenly.

3. Beat the eggs; add the grated cheese and seasoning; pour mixture carefully into the flan case.

4. Bake at 400°F/205°C (Gas Mark 6) for 10 minutes, then reduce heat to 350°F/180°C (Gas Mark 4) and cook flan for 20 minutes more, or until egg filling is set. Serve hot or cold.

CHICORY FLAN
(Russian Style)

Pastry to line an 8 in. flan dish
3 large heads of chicory
1 large onion
½ small fennel bulb
2 oz (50 g) polyunsaturated margarine
1 oz (25 g) plain wholemeal flour
½ pt (275 ml) milk
4 tablespoonsful thick plain yogurt
Seasoning to taste

1. Roll out the pastry to line a flan dish. Set aside.

2. Remove any discoloured leaves from the chicory, cut off base, then chop into pieces.

3. Slice the onion and the fennel.

4. Cook all the vegetables gently in 1 oz of the margarine, stirring frequently, for about 15 minutes. Remove from heat.

5. Make a white sauce: melt the rest of the margarine in a pan, stir in the sifted flour and *sauté* until slightly browned, then add the milk and cook until sauce thickens. Season well.

6. Add the yogurt to the sauce and stir, then add the drained vegetables.

7. Pile the mixture into the flan case, smooth the top, and bake at 400°F/205°C (Gas Mark 6) for 30 minutes, or until pastry is crisp. Serve hot.

CURD CHEESE AND CAULIFLOWER QUICHE

Pastry to line an 8 in. flan dish
½ a medium cauliflower
8 oz (225 g) curd cheese
1 oz (25 g) plain wholemeal flour
¼ pt (150 ml) milk
2 eggs, separated
1-2 oz (25-50 g) Cheddar cheese
Good pinch grated nutmeg
Seasoning to taste

1. Line the flan dish with the rolled out pastry, and bake for 10 minutes at 400°F/205°C (Gas Mark 6). Remove from oven and set aside to cool slightly.

2. Cut the stalks from the cauliflower and break the head into small florets; steam gently until tender but not mushy. Drain, then lay them across base of flan.

3. Sieve the curd cheese; blend it with the milk, flour, egg yolks, and seasoning.

4. Beat the egg whites until stiff, then fold them into the cheese. Spoon the mixture into the flan case, and top with the grated Cheddar cheese and nutmeg.

5. Bake at 350°F/180°C (Gas Mark 4) for about 45 minutes, or until set. Serve hot.

RED PEPPER FLAN

For Pastry
2 oz (50 g) cream cheese
8 oz (225 g) plain wholemeal flour
2 oz (50 g) polyunsaturated margarine
Approx. 2 tablespoonsful water
Squeeze of lemon juice

For Filling
3 medium red peppers
1 medium onion
2 tablespoonsful vegetable oil
4 oz (100 g) walnuts, hazelnuts or almonds
4 oz (100 g) wholemeal breadcrumbs
1 large egg
Approx. 4 tablespoonsful creamy milk
1 teaspoonful mixed herbs
Parsley
Seasoning to taste

1. Make the pastry by cutting the margarine and cream cheese into the flour with a knife, then using fingers to rub in the fats until the mixture resembles fine crumbs.

2. Add lemon juice and just enough water to make the dough smooth and non-crumbly. Knead briefly, then wrap in aluminium or cling foil and cool in the fridge for at least 30 minutes.

3. Slice the peppers and onion, and *sauté* in the vegetable oil until just beginning to brown; add the bread crumbs and cook a few minutes more; remove pan from heat.

4. Coarsely chop the nuts, and add to the mixture with the herbs and seasoning, stirring well.

5. Beat in the egg, and enough milk to make the mixture soft, but not too moist.

6. Spoon into the prepared flan case and bake at 375°F/190°C (Gas Mark 5) for 30 minutes, or until pastry is golden, and filling is set. Serve hot, garnished with chopped parsley.

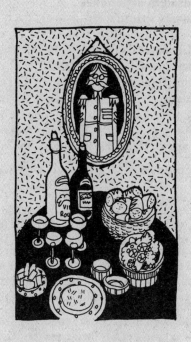

WINTER VEGETABLE FLAN

For Base
4 oz (100g) wholewheat crackers or crispbread
4 oz (100g) polyunsaturated margarine
4 oz (100g) flaked peanuts
Seasoning to taste

For Filling
½ a small red cabbage
8 oz (225g) Jerusalem artichokes
8 oz (225g) brussels sprouts
1 large onion
2 tablespoonsful vegetable oil
3 tablespoonsful peanut butter
1 teaspoonful miso (soya bean *purée*), or to taste
Seasoning to taste

1. Make a crumbly mixture of the crackers; rub in the margarine; stir in the flaked peanuts.

2. Press the mixture into a lightly greased 8 in. flan dish and bake blind at 400°F/205°C (Gas Mark 6) for about 20 minutes. Set aside to cool.

3. Meanwhile, *sauté* the sliced cabbage, artichokes and onion in the oil for 10 minutes, stirring frequently.

4. Pour in a little water in which the miso has been dissolved; add the cleaned, quartered brussels sprouts; simmer the vegetables for 20 minutes more, or until tender.

5. Stir in the peanut butter and seasoning, blend well, then spoon the mixture evenly into the flan case.

6. Return flan to oven and heat through for just 5-10 minutes at 350°F/180°C (Gas Mark 4). (If the flan case is cooked at the same time as the vegetables, and is still warm, you can, if you prefer, just fill it with the vegetable mixture and serve straight away.)

SOUFFLÉ QUICHE

Pastry to line an 8 in. flan dish
4 oz (100g) mushrooms
1 tablespoonful vegetable oil
1 oz (25g) plain wholemeal flour, with bran sifted out
1 oz (25g) polyunsaturated margarine
2 eggs, separated
2 oz (50g) grated Cheddar cheese
1/3 pt (200ml) milk
Pinch of cayenne pepper
Seasoning to taste

1. Roll out the pastry and line the flan dish, then bake blind for 10 minutes at 400°F/205°C (Gas Mark 6).

2. Heat the oil and lightly *sauté* the cleaned, sliced mushrooms, then drain well on a paper towel.

3. Melt the margarine in a pan, add the flour and cook for a minute. Remove from heat.

4. Stir in the milk gradually, then return to heat and bring to the boil, stirring continually, until the sauce thickens.

5. Cool for a minute or two, then stir in the egg yolks, mushroom slices, grated cheese, cayenne pepper and seasoning.

6. Whisk the egg whites until stiff and fold them carefully into the mixture.

7. Pour into the flan case. Bake at 375°F/190°C (Gas Mark 5) for 20-30 minutes, or until the *soufflé* has risen. Serve immediately.

ONION FLAN MORNAY

Pastry to line an 8 in. flan dish
4 medium onions
1 medium green pepper
1 tablespoonful vegetable oil
1 oz (25 g) polyunsaturated margarine
1 oz (25 g) plain wholemeal flour
¼ pt (150 ml) milk
¼ pt (150 ml) soured cream
2 oz (50 g) Cheddar cheese
1-2 oz (25-50 g) wholemeal breadcrumbs
Good pinch of sage (preferably fresh)
Seasoning to taste

1. Roll out pastry and use to line a flan dish. Bake blind at 400°F/205°C (Gas Mark 6) for 10 minutes.

2. Meanwhile, lightly *sauté* the sliced onions and pepper together in the vegetable oil. Drain well.

3. Heat the margarine and add the flour, stirring until it browns. Remove from heat and pour in the milk, then return to cooker and bring to the boil, still stirring.

4. When sauce thickens, remove pan from heat once more and blend in the sour cream. Add the vegetables, chopped sage and seasoning, mixing thoroughly.

5. Spoon the vegetables and sauce into the flan dish; sprinkle with the grated Cheddar cheese and bread crumbs.

6. Bake at 400°F/205°C (Gas Mark 6) until pastry is cooked, which will probably take about 20 minutes more. Serve hot.

PEPERONATA QUICHE

For Quiche
Pastry to line an 8 in. flan dish
½ pt (275 ml) milk
2 eggs
3 oz (75 g) Cheddar cheese
Seasoning to taste

For Peperonata Topping
2 large green peppers
1 large onion
4 large tomatoes
1 tablespoonful vegetable oil
1 oz (25 g) polyunsaturated margarine
Seasoning to taste

1. Line a flan dish with the prepared pastry.

2. Beat together the eggs and milk; add the grated cheese and seasoning; pour into the flan case.

3. Bake at 375°F/190°C (Gas Mark 5) for about 30 minutes.

4. Meanwhile, heat the oil and margarine together, then *sauté* the sliced onion in the fat.

5. Seed, core, and cut the peppers into strips; add to the onions and cook covered for 10 minutes.

6. Quarter the tomatoes and add to the pan with seasoning.

7. Continue to cook uncovered until most of the liquid has evaporated, and the vegetables are tender. Stir frequently.

8. When quiche is ready, spread the peperonata mixture evenly across the top of it, and serve immediately.

AVOCADO FLAN
(Cold)

For Base
6 oz (175 g) wholewheat cereal
3 oz (75 g) polyunsaturated margarine
2 oz (50 g) Cheddar cheese

For Filling
2 large ripe avocados
1 teaspoonful lemon juice
4 hard-boiled eggs
½ a clove of garlic, finely chopped
1 teaspoonful chives, finely chopped
1 teaspoonful parsley, finely chopped
2-3 tablespoonsful mayonnaise
Pinch of paprika
Seasoning to taste
Watercress to garnish

1. Crumble the wholewheat cereal; rub in the fat; stir in the grated cheese.

2. Press the mixture firmly and evenly against the base and sides of an 8 in. flan dish, and bake blind at 350°F/180°C (Gas Mark 4) for 15 minutes. Set aside to cool.

3. Cut the avocados in half, scoop out the flesh, and use a fork to mash it to a smooth *purée* with the lemon juice.

4. Mash the eggs, then combine them with the avocado *purée*, garlic, chives, parsley and mayonnaise. Keep on blending the ingredients in this way until you have a thick, creamy mixture.

5. Season to taste, then spoon into the prepared flan case and smooth the top.

6. Garnish with the paprika and watercress, and serve at once, or chill in the refrigerator until needed.

Note: If you prefer not to use eggs (or just wish to try a different version of this recipe) replace them with 6-8 oz (175-225 g) cottage cheese.

TOMATO AND PASTA FLAN

Pastry to line an 8 in. flan dish
1 large onion
1 clove garlic, crushed
2 large sticks celery
1 14 oz (400g) tin of tomatoes (or fresh equivalent)
Pinch of demerara raw cane sugar
1 tablespoonful oregano
2 tablespoonsful vegetable oil
3 oz (75g) wholewheat spaghetti rings
4 oz (100g) bel paese or mozzarella cheese
10 green olives with stones removed
Seasoning to taste

1. Roll out pastry and line flan dish; bake blind at 400°F/205°C (Gas Mark 6) for 20 minutes.

2. Heat the oil in a saucepan; add the onion, garlic and finely chopped celery, and cook for 10 minutes over a low heat.

3. Tip in the tomatoes, stir to break them up, then add raw cane sugar, seasoning and herbs, and bring to the boil.

4. Cook the vegetables uncovered over a medium heat for 10-15 minutes, or until most of the liquid has dried up.

5. Meanwhile, bring a pan of water to the boil and add the wholewheat spaghetti rings; cook for about 10 minutes, then drain well.

6. Put half the cheese, finely sliced, on the base of the flan.

7. Combine the tomato *purée* and pasta, stir in the coarsely chopped olives, and spoon the mixture evenly into the flan case.

8. Top with the rest of the cheese.

9. Return to the oven at 325°F/165°C (Gas Mark 3) for 10-15 minutes, or until the pastry is cooked. Serve hot.

Note: If using fresh tomatoes, you will need about 1½ lb (675 g), and they should be skinned and chopped – you may need to add extra water. Although fresh foods are always better than tinned, the Italian tomatoes do have a different taste that is better suited to the traditional sauce. On the other hand, local tomatoes will also, of course, produce a delicious sauce. The choice is yours.

CURRIED SPINACH AND LENTIL FLAN

Pastry to line an 8 in. flan dish
1 lb (450g) fresh or frozen spinach
8 oz (225g) small red lentils, pre-soaked
2 tablespoonsful vegetable oil
1 large onion
1 clove of garlic, crushed
1 teaspoonful ground coriander
1 teaspoonful garam masala
½ teaspoonful ground cumin
Sea salt to taste

1. Roll out the pastry; line a flan dish; bake blind at 400°F/205°C (Gas Mark 6) for 10 minutes.

2. Heat the oil in a pan and *sauté* the sliced onion and garlic for a few minutes, then add the lentils with just enough water to cover them, and cook thoroughly for about 20 minutes, or until tender. Drain off excess liquid.

3. Chop the well washed spinach, and add to the lentils with the salt, coriander, cumin and garam masala.

4. Cover and cook gently for just a few minutes more.

5. Spoon the spinach and lentils into the flan case; smooth the top; and bake at 350°F/180°C (Gas Mark 4) for 20 minutes more, or until flan case is cooked. Serve hot.

GREEN BEAN QUICHE

Pastry to line an 8 in. flan dish
8 oz (225 g) fresh or frozen green beans
1 oz (25 g) polyunsaturated margarine
1 oz (25 g) plain wholemeal flour, with bran sifted out
Approx. ¼ pt (150 ml) milk
2 eggs
2 oz (50 g) grated Parmesan cheese
2 oz wholewheat cereal
Pinch of nutmeg
Seasoning to taste

1. Line the flan dish with the rolled out pastry. Set aside.

2. Slice the beans and steam them, or cook in the minimum amount of water, until tender. Drain.

3. Make a thick white sauce by melting the margarine in a pan, adding the flour and cooking briefly, then stirring in the milk and cooking gently for a few minutes longer.

4. Cool the sauce slightly, then add the beaten eggs, grated cheese, nutmeg and seasoning, and finally the green beans.

5. Combine well, then spoon the mixture into the flan case and smooth the top.

6. Sprinkle with the crumbled wholewheat cereal, then bake at 375°F/190°C (Gas Mark 5) for about 40 minutes, or until filling is set. Serve hot or cold.

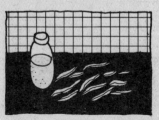

BRUSSELS SPROUTS FLAN WITH BLUE CHEESE

Pastry to line an 8 in. flan dish
Approx. 1 lb (450g) brussels sprouts, fresh or frozen
1 large onion, minced as finely as possible
1 large red pepper, cut into strips
2 oz (50g) polyunsaturated margarine
2 oz (50g) blue cheese
2 oz (50g) roasted peanuts

1. Roll out pastry and line flan dish.

2. Wash brussels sprouts, remove tough stems and discoloured outer leaves; steam, or cook with the minimum of water, until tender.

2. Meanwhile, melt the margarine and *sauté* strips of pepper until just beginning to brown. Drain on paper towel.

4. In the same pan, cook the minced onion for a few minutes.

5. Add the crumbled blue cheese and stir until it melts.

6. Chop the cooked brussels sprouts coarsely, and add to the cheese and onion mixture; stir in the peanuts.

7. Spoon mixture into the flan case and spread evenly. Garnish with the strips of pepper.

8. Bake at 400°F/205°C (Gas Mark 6) for 20 minutes or until pastry is crisp and golden. Serve hot.

PARSNIP FLAN

For Base
4 oz (100g) rolled oats
2 oz (50g) plain wholemeal flour
2 tablespoonsful vegetable oil
Seasoning to taste

For Filling
1 lb (450g) parsnips
2 oz (50g) Cheddar cheese
2 eggs
1 oz (25g) sunflower seeds
Pinch of nutmeg, preferably freshly grated
Seasoning to taste

1. Mix together the oats and flour; season; stir in the oil.

2. Add a little water and mix well to make a firm dough, then press it evenly against the sides and base of the flan dish.

3. Peel, chop, and steam the parsnips until soft enough to mash.

4. Combine the *purée* with the grated cheese, beaten eggs, nutmeg and seasoning, and spoon into the flan case.

5. Scatter with the sunflower seeds.

6. Bake at 400°F/205°C (Gas Mark 6) for 30 minutes, when egg filling should be set.

QUICHE LORRAINE

Pastry to line an 8 in. flan dish
½ pt (275 ml) single cream or ¼ pt (150 ml) milk, ¼ pt
   (150 ml) single cream
3 eggs
4 oz (100 g) Gruyère cheese
3 tablespoonsful soya 'bacon' pieces
Pinch of grated nutmeg
Seasoning to taste

1. Roll out the pastry and line a dish, turning the pastry so it is twice as thick on the sides.

2. Scatter soya 'bacon' over the bottom of the pastry.

3. Beat together the cream and eggs, add the grated cheese, and season well.

4. Pour egg mixture into the flan case, then bake at 400°F/205°C (Gas Mark 6) for 30-35 minutes. Serve hot or cold.

Note: As this is a very liquid filling, you may prefer to bake the pastry blind for 10 minutes at 400°F/205°C (Gas Mark 6) before pouring in the egg mixture.

ADUKI BEAN FLAN

Pastry to line an 8 in. flan dish
8 oz (225 g) aduki beans, soaked overnight
2 large onions
2 tablespoonsful vegetable oil
2 teaspoonsful mixed herbs
Soy sauce to taste
Seasoning to taste
Parsley to garnish

1. Line a flan dish with the pastry; prick the dough; bake blind for 15 minutes at 400°F/205°C (Gas Mark 6).

2. Cook the aduki beans in water until very soft.

3. Drain, then mash or blend the beans to a firm *purée*.

4. Slice the onions, then *sauté* in the heated oil so that they begin to brown.

5. Combine thoroughly the beans, onions, herbs, seasoning, and a dash of soy sauce.

6. Spoon into the part-cooked flan case and garnish with the chopped parsley.

7. Continue to bake for 15 minutes more, or until pastry is cooked. Serve hot.

PUMPKIN FLAN

For Pastry
Pastry to line an 8 in. flan dish
1 tablespoonful grated onion

For Filling
Approx. 1½ lb (675 g) pumpkin
2 medium tomatoes
2 eggs
1 large onion
1 tablespoonful vegetable oil
Good pinch of nutmeg
Seasoning to taste

1. Make pastry according to basic instructions, but add grated onion and distribute evenly.

2. Roll out and use to line a flan dish, then bake blind at 400°F/205°C (Gas Mark 6) for 10 minutes.

3. Slice the tomatoes and layer them evenly across the flan base.

4. Peel the pumpkin, chop the flesh into cubes, and steam until soft.

5. *Sauté* the peeled, sliced onion in the oil for a few minutes, then combine with the well mashed pumpkin and seasoning. Cool mixture slightly.

6. Add beaten eggs. (If a lighter-textured flan is preferred, add the egg yolks first, then beat the egg whites until stiff before folding into the mixture.)

7. Pour the *purée* into the flan case and bake at 375°F/190°C (Gas Mark 5) for 30 minutes or until set. Serve hot.

BROCCOLI QUICHE IN RICE CASE

For Base
6 oz (175 g) cooked brown rice, well drained

For Filling
8 oz (225 g) fresh or frozen broccoli
½ pt (275 ml) milk
2 eggs
4 oz (100 g) Cheshire cheese
Grated nutmeg
Seasoning to taste

1. Grease an 8 in. flan dish lightly, then use the back of a metal spoon to press the rice firmly against the base and sides of the dish.

2. Bake at 350°F/180°C (Gas Mark 4) for 5 to 10 minutes, or until crisp.

3. Remove the stalks from the broccoli, and gently steam the florets until cooked. Cool, then scatter in rice case.

4. Beat the eggs, then combine with the milk, crumbled or grated cheese and seasoning. Pour over the broccoli.

5. Sprinkle grated nutmeg over flan, then bake at 375°F/190°C (Gas Mark 5) for 30 minutes.

LENTIL FLAN

Pastry to line an 8 in. flan dish
4 oz (100 g) small red lentils
1/3 pt (200 ml) milk and water mixed (or water with 2
    tablespoonsful skimmed milk powder)
1 large onion
1 tablespoonful vegetable oil
1 teaspoonful mixed herbs
1 teaspoonful yeast extract
1 egg
Seasoning to taste

1. Line a flan dish with the pastry.

2. Heat the oil and *sauté* the sliced onion for a few minutes.

3. Add the lentils and liquid, and cook thoroughly for 15
    minutes or until lentils are soft. Drain off any liquid that has
    not been absorbed.

4. Mix the lentils with the herbs, seasoning, yeast extract, and
    beaten egg.

5. Pour into the flan case and bake at 350°F/180°C (Gas Mark
    4) for about 45 minutes, when the filling should be quite
    firm. Serve hot or cold.

CLIVE BIRCH

QUICK YOGURT QUICHE

For Base
6 oz (175g) wholewheat crackers or crispbread
4 oz (100g) polyunsaturated margarine

For Topping
1 small carton plain yogurt
3 eggs
¼ pt (150ml) milk or cream
3 oz (75g) Cheddar cheese
½ small cucumber
Seasoning to taste
Chives

1. Crush the crackers and combine well with the melted margarine, then press the mixture firmly into the base of an 8 in. flan dish.

2. Whisk the eggs, add the yogurt and milk, season well.

3. Grate the cheese and stir it into the mixture.

4. Slice the cucumber and layer it across the base of the prepared flan; pour in the liquid mixture; top with chopped chives.

5. Bake at 350°F/180°C (Gas Mark 4) for about 30 minutes, or until filling is set. Serve hot or cold.

SWISS CHARD, TOMATO AND TOFU FLAN

Pastry to line an 8 in. flan dish
8 oz (225g) Swiss chard
1 onion or 3 spring onions
2 celery sticks
2 tomatoes
4 oz (100g) tofu (bean curd)
2 tablespoonsful vegetable oil
1-2 tablespoonsful sesame seeds
Soy sauce to taste
Seasoning to taste

1. Use the rolled out pastry to line a flan dish.

2. Heat the oil in a frying pan and *sauté* the chopped onion with the finely sliced celery sticks.

3. Drain and coarsely mash the tofu; add to the pan and *sauté* briefly.

4. Sprinkle in some soy sauce, then tear the Swiss chard into bite sized pieces and add to the pan, mixing it with the other ingredients.

5. Chop the tomatoes coarsely and put in the pan.

6. Cook gently for 5 minutes, adding a little water if necessary, until the Swiss chard begins to wilt.

7. Spoon the mixture evenly into the prepared flan case (drain off any surplus liquid); smooth the top, and sprinkle with sesame seeds.

8. Bake at 400°F/205°C (Gas Mark 6) for 10 minutes, then at 350°F/180°C (Gas Mark 4) for 20 minutes more, or until pastry crust is crisp. Serve hot or warm.

AUBERGINE FLAN

Pastry to line an 8 in. flan dish
2 medium aubergines
4 eggs
4 tablespoonsful milk
Approx. 2 oz (50g) plain wholemeal flour
1 oz (25g) wheat germ
1-2 teaspoonsful marjoram
Parsley
Seasoning to taste

1. Top, tail and peel the aubergines; slice thinly lengthwise; lay on a dish and sprinkle with salt. Set aside to drain for at least 30 minutes.

2. Roll out pastry and use to line a flan dish; bake blind at 400°F/205°C (Gas Mark 6) for 10 minutes.

3. Rinse aubergine slices in cold water and pat dry with a paper towel.

4. Sift together the flour and wheat germ, then dip each slice of aubergine into the mixture, shaking off the excess.

5. Heat the oil and fry the aubergine slices on both sides. Drain well.

6. Arrange the aubergine slices across the base of the flan case.

7. Beat the eggs; add the milk, marjoram, finely chopped parsley and seasoning.

8. Pour liquid mixture into the flan case and bake at 375°F/190°C (Gas Mark 5) for 20 minutes, or until set. Serve hot.

CABBAGE FLAN WITH CHICK PEAS

Pastry to line an 8 in. flan dish
4 oz (100g) cooked chick peas
½ small white cabbage
4 medium carrots
2 medium onions
2 tablespoonsful vegetable oil
2 tablespoonsful tahini (sesame spread)
1 teaspoonful lemon juice
1 clove garlic, crushed
Seasoning to taste
Parsley or tomato slices

1.   Roll out pastry and use to line flan dish. Bake blind at 400°F/205°C (Gas Mark 6) for 10 minutes.

2.   Heat the oil in a large pan and gently *sauté* the sliced onions with the garlic for a few minutes.

3.   Add the finely sliced carrots and cook for 5 minutes; stir in the shredded cabbage, and continue cooking over a low heat for 5 minutes more.

4.   Cover the pan and simmer for just a little longer, or until the vegetables are tender but still crisp.

5.   Stir in the drained chick peas as they are, or coarsely grind or chop them first.

6.   Add the lemon juice, tahini and seasoning; cook mixture briefly until most of the moisture has dried up.

7.   Spoon into the flan case and bake at 350°F/180°C (Gas Mark 4) for 15 minutes, or until the pastry is cooked. Serve hot, garnished with chopped parsley or tomato slices (or both).

COTTAGE CHEESE AND TOMATO QUICHE

Pastry to line an 8 in. flan dish
2 large tomatoes
1 large onion
1 oz (25 g) polyunsaturated margarine or vegetable oil
8 oz (225 g) cottage cheese
3 eggs
Parsley
Seasoning to taste

1. Roll out pastry and line flan dish.

2. Heat the margarine and lightly fry the sliced onions, then remove from heat and drain on a paper towel.

3. Slice the tomatoes and layer them across the base of the flan.

4. Mix together the beaten eggs, sieved cottage cheese, onion, parsley and seasoning, then pour onto the tomato slices.

5. Bake the quiche at 400°F/205°C (Gas Mark 6) for 15 minutes, then reduce heat to 350°F/180°C (Gas Mark 4) and cook for a further 30 minutes, or until set.

RATATOUILLE FLAN WITH CHEESE PASTRY

For Pastry
4 oz (100g) grated cheese
8 oz (225g) plain wholemeal flour
3 oz (75g) polyunsaturated margarine
Approx. 2 tablespoonsful water
Pinch of sea salt

For Filling
1 medium aubergine
1 medium green pepper
3 medium courgettes
2 large tomatoes
2 large onions
½-1 clove garlic, crushed
2 tablespoonsful vegetable oil
Seasoning to taste

1. To make the pastry: rub the margarine into the flour to make a crumb-like mixture, then use a knife to blend in the grated cheese.

2. Add enough water to make a medium soft dough; wrap in aluminium or cling foil and leave in the fridge for half an hour.

3. To make the ratatouille: top and tail the aubergine and cut into cubes; slice the pepper, courgettes, tomatoes and onions.

4. Heat the oil and gently fry the onion and crushed garlic for a few minutes; then add all the other vegetables, cover the pan, and simmer for about 30 minutes.

5. Roll out the pastry and line an 8 in. flan dish.

6. Bake blind for 10 minutes at 400°F/205°C (Gas Mark 6).

7. Season the vegetables, then spoon them into the flan base, draining off the excess liquid; return flan to the oven for 20 minutes more so that the pastry is completely cooked. Serve hot.

Note: For a more filling flan add 2 beaten eggs to the ratatouille before putting the mixture into the flan case, and cook until set.

SPINACH FLAN

Pastry to line an 8 in. flan dish
1 lb (450g) fresh or frozen spinach
1 oz (25g) sultanas, plumped up in boiling water
1 oz (25g) pine nuts
2 tablespoonsful olive or vegetable oil
2 oz (50g) grated Parmesan cheese
Parsley
Pinch of nutmeg
Seasoning to taste

1. Roll out the prepared pastry and line a flan dish, then bake blind at 400°F/205°C (Gas Mark 6) for 10 minutes.

2. Meanwhile, wash the spinach carefully, then steam or cook in the minimum amount of water until tender. Drain very well and squeeze dry.

3. Heat the oil in a pan and add the coarsely chopped spinach, pine nuts, and the sultanas, then cook gently for a few minutes, stirring frequently.

4. Stir in some fresh parsley, a little nutmeg, and seasoning; spoon mixture into the flan case; top with the Parmesan cheese.

5. Return flan to the oven and cook for 20 minutes more at 350°F/180°C (Gas Mark 4), when pastry should be cooked. Serve hot.

SCRAMBLED EGG FLAN

Pastry to line an 8 in. flan dish
6 eggs
1 oz (25g) polyunsaturated margarine
3 tablespoonsful cream or milk
1 small red pepper
2 oz (50g) mushrooms
2 oz (50g) peas, fresh or frozen
Seasoning to taste
Parsley

1. Roll out the prepared pastry and line flan dish; bake blind at 400°F/205°C (Gas Mark 6) for 20-30 minutes, or until pastry is crisp and golden.

2. Meanwhile, cook the peas in a little water. Drain well.

3. Melt the margarine in a large pan and gently *sauté* the finely sliced pepper for 5 minutes; then add the chopped mushrooms and cook 5 minutes longer, stirring frequently.

4. Beat the eggs together with the cream, season to taste, and add to the pan.

5. Cook mixture on a low heat, stirring continually, until lightly set; remove from heat immediately, then leave to cool in the pan for 2 or 3 minutes more.

6. Stir in the hot peas.

7. Spoon egg and vegetable scramble into the warm flan case, smooth the top, sprinkle with coarsely chopped fresh parsley. Serve at once.

PEA AND POTATO QUICHE

Pastry to line an 8 in. flan dish
8 oz (225 g) potatoes
1 medium onion
1 tablespoonful vegetable oil
4 oz (100 g) fresh or frozen peas
3 eggs
½ pt (275 ml) milk
4 oz (100 g) Cheddar cheese
Pinch of paprika
Seasoning to taste

1. Line the flan dish with the rolled out pastry, and set aside.

2. Heat the oil and gently *sauté* the sliced onion, then remove from heat and drain on paper towel.

3. Chop the peeled potatoes into small cubes and boil together with the peas until both vegetables are tender. Drain well.

4. Mix the peas, potato cubes and onion, and distribute them evenly across the base of the flan.

5. Beat the eggs, combine with the milk and grated cheddar. Season well. Pour into the flan case and top with the paprika.

6. Bake at 375°F/190°C (Gas Mark 5) for 30 minutes, or until set. Serve hot.

TAHINI VEGETABLE FLAN

For Pastry
Pastry to line an 8 in. flan dish
2 tablespoonsful sesame seeds

For Filling
1 small cabbage
4 large carrots
2 large onions
2 large sticks celery
2 oz (50 g) peas, fresh or frozen
2 tablespoonsful vegetable oil
1-2 teaspoonsful mixed herbs
3 tablespoonsful tahini (sesame spread)
Soy sauce
Seasoning to taste

1. Add sesame seeds to pastry dough; roll out and line flan dish; bake blind for 15 minutes at 400°F/205°C (Gas Mark 6).

2. Cook the peas in a little water, then drain well.

3. Peel and slice the carrots and onions; shred the washed cabbage; chop up the celery sticks.

4. Heat the oil and stir-fry the prepared vegetables on a medium heat for about 5 minutes, making sure they do not burn.

5. Add the herbs and a sprinkling of soy sauce and turn the heat low; cover the pan and cook the vegetables for 10 minutes more. (You may need to add a spoonful of water.)

6. Stir in the peas and seasoning; add the tahini and blend well until the vegetables are covered in a thick creamy sauce.

7. Pour into the flan case and bake at 350°F/180°C (Gas Mark 4) for 15 minutes, or until pastry is cooked. Serve hot.

SAGE DERBY QUICHE

Pastry to line an 8 in. flan dish
1-2 teaspoonsful sage
3 eggs
3 oz (75 g) Cheddar cheese
3 oz (75 g) sage Derby cheese
1/3 pt (200 ml) creamy milk
Seasoning to taste

1. Add the herbs to the pastry, then roll out and use to line the flan dish. Set aside.

2. Beat the eggs well, add the grated Cheddar cheese, milk and seasoning and combine thoroughly.

3. Grate or crumble the sage Derby cheese and spread across the base of the prepared flan.

4. Pour in the egg mixture.

5. Bake at 400°F/205°C (Gas Mark 6) for about 30 minutes. Serve hot or cold.

CELERY FLAN AMANDINE

For Base
2 oz (50 g) ground almonds
4 oz (100 g) plain wholemeal flour
3 oz (75 g) polyunsaturated margarine
Cold water to mix

For Filling
1 large head of celery
1 small onion
2 oz (50 g) polyunsaturated margarine
1 oz (25 g) plain wholemeal flour
½ pt (275 ml) cream or creamy milk
3-4 oz (75-100 g) roasted flaked almonds
Seasoning to taste

1. Combine the flour and ground almonds, then rub in the margarine.

2. Add enough water to make a firm dough; knead briefly, then wrap in aluminium or cling foil and chill in the fridge.

3. Roll out the chilled pastry, line a flan dish, and bake blind for 20 minutes at 400°F/205°C (Gas Mark 6). Cool slightly.

4. Clean the celery and slice diagonally in small pieces; chop the onion as finely as possible; cook celery and onion in the melted margarine for 10-15 minutes, stirring occasionally.

5. When celery is just tender, sprinkle in the flour, add the cream and stir to make a thick sauce. Remove from heat.

6. Spoon the mixture into the flan case, smooth the top, and scatter generously with the nuts.

7. Bake at 350°F/180°C (Gas Mark 4) for about 10 minutes more. Serve hot.

COURGETTE QUICHE

Pastry to line an 8 in. flan dish
1 oz (25 g) polyunsaturated margarine
1 large onion
2 medium courgettes
¼ pt (150 ml) cream or creamy milk
1 egg
2 more egg yolks
2 oz (50 g) grated Parmesan cheese
Pinch of nutmeg
Seasoning to taste

1. Roll out pastry, line the flan dish, and bake blind at 400°F/205°C (Gas Mark 6) for 10 minutes.

2. Melt the margarine in a pan and briefly *sauté* the chopped onion before adding the thinly sliced courgettes. Continue cooking gently for 5 minutes, stirring occasionally.

3. Spoon the vegetables into the slightly cooled flan case.

4. Beat together the egg, egg yolks, cream, nutmeg and seasoning, and pour over the vegetables. Sprinkle with cheese.

5. Bake at 350°F/180°C (Gas Mark 4) for 30 minutes, or until set. Serve hot.

SWEET CORN FLAN WITH YOGURT

Pastry to line an 8 in. flan dish
Approx. 14 oz (400g) sweet corn – fresh or frozen
3 oz (75g) wholemeal breadcrumbs
1 large egg
2 small cartons plain yogurt
1 teaspoonful basil
Chives to garnish
Seasoning to taste

1. Use the pastry to line a flan dish, and set aside.

2. Cook and drain the sweet corn, then cool slightly.

3. In a bowl mix together thoroughly the sweet corn, breadcrumbs, beaten egg, yogurt, basil and seasoning.

4. Spoon the mixture into the flan case; smooth the top.

5. Bake at 400°F/205°C (Gas Mark 6) for 30 minutes. Serve hot, garnished with the chopped chives.

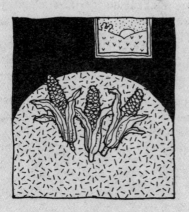

CHESTNUT AND BRUSSELS FLAN

Pastry to line an 8 in. flan dish
6 oz (175 g) small brussels sprouts
3 oz (75 g) dried chestnuts or 5 oz (150g) fresh chestnuts
1 oz (25 g) polyunsaturated margarine
1 oz (25 g) wholemeal flour
3 oz (75 g) Cheddar cheese
1 small onion
Seasoning to taste
1 teaspoonful marjoram

1. Use the prepared pastry to line a flan dish and set aside.

2. Hydrate the dried chestnuts; if using fresh, slit the skins and boil steadily for 10 minutes to remove outside and inside skins.

3. Boil the chestnuts for 15-30 minutes, or until just softening.

4. Trim the outer leaves and stems from the brussels sprouts; wash, then steam for 10 minutes. If using large ones, cut them in half.

5. In a frying pan, melt the margarine and gently *sauté* the slices of onion; sprinkle in the flour and cook until golden.

6. Add enough cold water (or the water from the brussels sprouts pan) to make a thick sauce, stirring continuously; stir in the grated cheese, seasoning and marjoram.

7. Mix the drained brussels sprouts and chestnuts with the sauce and spoon into the flan case; bake at 400°F/205°C (Gas Mark 6) for 10 minutes, then at 350°F/180°C (Gas Mark 4) for about 20 minutes longer, or until the pastry is cooked.

CURRIED EGG FLAN

Pastry to line an 8 in. flan dish
6 hard-boiled eggs
1 medium onion
1 medium apple
½ clove crushed garlic
1 oz (25 g) wholemeal flour
2 oz (50 g) polyunsaturated margarine or 2 tablespoonsful
  vegetable oil
1 teaspoonful curry powder
1 teaspoonful curry paste
2 large tomatoes, skinned or 1 tablespoonful tomato *purée*
¼ pt (150 ml) vegetable stock or water
1 oz (25 g) raisins
Squeeze of lemon juice
Seasoning to taste

1. Line the flan dish with the rolled out pastry and bake blind for 20 minutes at 375°F/190°C (Gas Mark 5).

2. Halve the eggs and arrange them across the base of the flan, cut side down.

3. Heat the fat and cook the sliced onion and garlic slowly for 5 minutes; add the curry powder and paste and cook for 10 more minutes, stirring now and again.

4. Add the flour and when it has absorbed the fat, stir in the water and bring to the boil to make a smooth thick sauce.

5. Add the finely chopped apple, tomatoes, raisins, lemon juice and seasoning; cook gently, covered, for 30 minutes.

6. Allow the curry sauce to cool slightly, then pour it into the flan case to cover the eggs as evenly as possible; heat through in the oven for 10 minutes, or until the pastry is cooked. Serve hot.

RICE SALAD FLAN

Pastry to line an 8 in. flan dish
3 oz (75 g) cooked brown rice
3 spring onions
¼ cucumber
8 radishes
Small bunch watercress
2 sticks celery
3 firm tomatoes
1 oz (25 g) chopped walnuts
2 oz (50 g) cream or curd cheese
2-4 tablespoonsful mayonnaise
Seasoning to taste
Paprika

1. Line a flan dish with the prepared pastry, and bake blind at 375°F/190°C (Gas Mark 5) for 25-30 minutes, or until completely cooked; set aside until cold.

2. In a bowl mix the rice with all the salad ingredients, retaining a few sprigs of watercress for a garnish.

3. Mix together the cheese and mayonnaise and stir into the rice salad; adjust the mayonnaise to taste, and to make the mixture moist without being too wet.

4. Season; stir in the chopped nuts, spoon into the flan case and smooth the top; garnish and sprinkle with a little paprika. Serve as soon as possible.

Note: Any salad ingredients can be used in this flan, and in whatever amount suits you and your family. Nuts, also, can be varied, but try always to include some of one kind or another as they add crunch as well as valuable protein.

CHILLI QUICHE

Pastry to line an 8 in. flan dish
3 oz (75 g) well cooked kidney beans
2 eggs
4 oz (100 g) Cheddar cheese
^{1}/$_3$ pt (180 ml) milk
1-2 teaspoonsful chilli powder (or to taste)

1. Make up the pastry and use to line the flan dish; bake blind for 10 minutes at 400°F/200°C (Gas Mark 6).

2. In a bowl, lightly beat the eggs; add the milk, grated cheese and chilli powder and blend thoroughly.

3. Stir in the well drained beans.

4. Pour the mixture into flan case, making sure the beans are evenly distributed; bake at the same temperature for 20 minutes more, or until the pastry is cooked and the filling set. Serve hot or cold.

LEEK AND CHEESE MERINGUE

For Pastry
7 oz (200g) plain wholemeal flour
3 oz (75g) polyunsaturated margarine
3 oz (75g) grated Cheddar cheese
1-2 tablespoonsful caraway seeds
Approx. 4 tablespoonsful water

For Filling
8 oz (225g) leeks
1 tablespoonful vegetable oil

For Topping
2 egg whites
2 oz (50g) grated Cheddar cheese
Seasoning to taste

1. To make the pastry, rub the margarine lightly into the flour, add the cheese, then enough water to bind to a dough.

2. Sprinkle with the seeds, knead lightly, then wrap and leave in the cool for at least 30 minutes.

3. Roll out the pastry and line the flan dish; bake blind at 375°F/190°C (Gas Mark 5) for 20 minutes.

4. Meanwhile, clean and chop the leeks into 1 in. segments, then *sauté* briefly in the oil; sprinkle with water, cover the pan, and cook gently until just tender.

5. Make the meringue topping by whisking the egg whites and seasoning until stiff, then folding in the grated cheese.

6. Arrange the drained leeks in the flan case; top with the meringue, and bake at 325°F/170°C (Gas Mark 3) for 20 minutes. Serve immediately.

CORNISH PASTY FLAN

Pastry to line an 8 in. flan dish
8 oz (225 g) potatoes
2 large onions
2 large carrots
2 tablespoonsful vegetable oil
3 oz (75 g) soya 'minced meat', hydrated
1 teaspoonful yeast extract, or to taste
Seasoning to taste

1. Peel and cube the potatoes and carrots; steam them until almost cooked.

2. Roll out the pastry and line the flan dish; bake blind for 15 minutes at 375°F/190°C (Gas Mark 5).

3. Heat the oil and lightly *sauté* the sliced onion with the soya 'meat'; stir in the yeast extract until completely dissolved; season, and add the potatoes and carrots. (If very dry, add a little vegetable stock.)

4. Spread the mixture across the base of the flan. Bake at 350°F/180°C (Gas Mark 4) for 10-15 minutes more, or until the pastry is cooked. Serve hot.

CREAMY VEGETABLE FLAN

For Base
6 oz (175 g) rolled oats
3 oz (75 g) polyunsaturated margarine
1 oz (25 g) sunflower seeds
Seasoning to taste

For Filling
Approx. 1 lb (450 g) mixed vegetables e.g. cauliflower florets, carrots, peas, green beans, courgettes, parsnips etc.
6 oz (175 g) cream cheese or curd cheese or a combination of both
Seasoning to taste

1. Use fingertips to rub the margarine into the oats; add the seeds and seasoning; press mixture down as evenly as possible to line the base and sides of a lightly greased flan dish.

2. Bake blind for 15 minutes at 400°F/200°C (Gas Mark 6).

3. Prepare the vegetables by cleaning and chopping them into small even-sized pieces; steam lightly until just tender.

4. Whilst the vegetables are still warm, stir in the cheese to make a creamy coating.

5. Spoon the vegetables into the flan case and return to the oven for 10-15 minutes more, or until the oat pastry is cooked.

CELERY CRUMBLE

Pastry to line an 8 in. flan dish
1 large celery
2 tablespoonsful vegetable oil
1 oz (25 g) plain wholemeal flour
¼ pt (150 ml) vegetable stock
1 teaspoonful miso, or to taste
Seasoning to taste
4 tablespoonsful millet flakes
1-2 tablespoonsful vegetable oil

1. Roll out the pastry, line a flan dish, and bake blind for 15 minutes at 400°F/200°C (Gas Mark 6).

2. Cut the celery into 1 in. pieces and cook gently, turning frequently in the oil.

3. Sprinkle in the flour and cook until just turning golden, then add the vegetable stock and bring to the boil, stirring until you have a smooth sauce.

4. Add the miso and seasoning.

5. Fill the flan case with the mixture and smooth the top.

6. Make the crumble by rubbing a little oil into the millet flakes with the fingertips, then season well and sprinkle over the top of the flan.

7. Return the flan to the oven; lower the heat to 350°F/180°C (Gas Mark 4), and cook for about 15 minutes more. Serve hot.

BROAD BEAN AND 'HAM' FLAN

Pastry to line an 8 in. flan dish
6 oz (175 g) shelled fresh broad beans or frozen equivalent
3 oz (75 g) soya 'ham' chunks, hydrated
1 oz (25 g) polyunsaturated margarine
1 oz (25 g) wholemeal flour
1/3 pt (180 ml) milk
Pinch of mixed herbs
Seasoning to taste

1. Line a flan with the prepared pastry and bake blind at 400°F/200°C (Gas Mark 6) for 25-30 minutes, or until cooked.

2. Meanwhile, cook the broad beans until just tender.

3. Heat the margarine in a pan and toss in the well drained 'ham' chunks; *sauté* for 5 minutes, stirring frequently.

4. Sprinkle in the flour and brown lightly before adding the milk; bring to the boil, stirring, to make a white sauce; add the seasoning and herbs.

5. Stir in the drained beans and heat through.

6. Spoon the mixture into the cooked flan case, smooth the top and serve immediately if desired, or return to the oven on a low heat for 5 minutes.

DUTCH FLAN

Pastry to line an 8 in. flan dish
4 oz (100g) Gouda cheese
2 large firm tomatoes
4 tablespoonsful soft wholemeal breadcrumbs
¼ pt (150 ml) milk
2 eggs
1-2 teaspoonsful mixed herbs
Seasoning to taste

1. Line a flan dish with the rolled out pastry and bake blind at 400°F/200°C (Gas Mark 6) for 10 minutes.

2. Put the crumbs into a bowl; bring the milk to a boil and pour over the crumbs; leave to stand for a few minutes before mixing thoroughly with a fork.

3. Add the beaten eggs, then the grated cheese; season and sprinkle in the herbs; mix again.

4. Slice the tomatoes and arrange them across the base of the flan; top with the mixture.

5. Bake at 350°F/180°C (Gas Mark 4) for 20-30 minutes, or until the filling is firm and the pastry crisp. Serve hot or cold.

CHILLED CUCUMBER FLAN

Pastry to line an 8in. flan dish
1 medium cucumber
4oz (100g) cream or curd cheese
2 heaped tablespoonsful mayonnaise, or to taste
4 teaspoonsful chervil, finely chopped
Seasoning to taste

1. Roll out the prepared pastry and line the flan dish; prick the base and bake blind at 400°F/200°C (Gas Mark 6) for 20 minutes, or until cooked.

2. Set the flan base aside to cool completely.

3. Mash the cheese until creamy smooth and mix with the finely chopped cucumber; season well; add enough mayonnaise to make the mixture soft but not too runny.

4. Mix in the chervil, retaining just a little; spoon the cucumber cheese into the pastry shell and smooth the top; sprinkle with the remaining chervil. (If liked, you could reserve a few wafer-thin slices of cucumber and garnish the flan with these.)

5. Chill before serving.

CLIVE BIRCH

QUICHE AU POIVRE

Pastry to line an 8in. flan dish
4 oz (100g) cream or curd cheese
1 oz (25g) polyunsaturated margarine
½ oz (15g) black peppercorns
½ pt (275 ml) creamy milk
3 egg yolks
Seasoning to taste

1. Line the flan dish with the prepared and rolled out pastry, and bake blind at 400°F/200°C (Gas Mark 6) for 10 minutes.

2. Meanwhile, crush the peppercorns coarsely and *sauté* them gently for just a few minutes in the melted margarine.

3. Remove the pan from the heat and leave to cool for a few minutes, then add the creamy milk into which you have whisked the egg yolks; blend well; season to taste.

4. Stir in the cream cheese until it dissolves. Pour the thick sauce into the partially cooked flan case.

5. Bake the flan at 400°F/200°C (Gas Mark 6) for 20-30 minutes, or until set.

CARROT FLAN

Pastry to line an 8in. flan dish
1lb (450g) carrots
½pt (275ml) vegetable stock
Pinch of raw cane sugar
2oz (50g) polyunsaturated margarine
2oz (50g) plain wholemeal flour
¼pt (150ml) single cream
3 eggs, separated
Seasoning to taste
Fresh savory

1. Roll out the pastry and line the flan dish.

2. Peel and slice the carrots, and cook in the vegetable stock and sugar for 15 minutes, or until very soft.

3. Drain the carrots, then mash them or *purée* them in a blender.

4. In a clean pan, melt the margarine, add the flour and *sauté* for a few minutes; pour in the cream and heat, stirring continually, to make a thick sauce.

5. Remove from the heat and allow to cool slightly; whisk in the carrot *purée* and egg yolks; season to taste.

6. Beat the egg whites until they hold their shape and then fold them into the other ingredients; spoon the mixture into the flan case and smooth the top.

7. Bake at 350°F/180°C (Gas Mark 4) for 30-45 minutes or until the carrot filling is set (test it with a knife). Serve hot, sprinkled with the chopped savory.

SAVOURY TOFU FLAN PROVENÇALE

Pastry to line an 8in. flan dish
1 small aubergine
1 onion
½-1 clove garlic, crushed
2oz (50g) mushrooms
4oz (100g) wholemeal breadcrumbs
4oz (100g) tofu
2oz (50g) sunflower seeds
4 tomatoes
2 tablespoonsful vegetable oil
Seasoning to taste

1. Line a dish with the prepared pastry and bake blind at 400°F/200°C (Gas Mark 6) for 10 minutes.

2. In a large pan, heat the oil and *sauté* the finely chopped onion and garlic for a few minutes.

3. Cut up the drained tofu and add to the pan, then mash it into the other ingredients and cook gently for a few minutes more.

4. Meanwhile, peel and cube the aubergine; add this to the pan and *sauté* briefly; add the sliced mushrooms, then sprinkle a tiny drop of water over the ingredients, cover the pan, and cook gently for 10 minutes.

5. Stir in the breadcrumbs and chopped tomatoes just long enough to absorb the flavours and any extra liquid; season; sprinkle in most of the sunflower seeds.

6. Transfer the mixture to the flan case and cook at 375°F/190°C (Gas Mark 5) for 15 minutes or until the pastry is cooked. Sprinkle with the remaining seeds for the last 5 minutes of cooking time.

SWEET FLANS

RICOTTA CHEESE FLAN

Pastry to line an 8 in. flan dish
12 oz (350g) ricotta cheese
2 tablespoonsful double cream
2 eggs
3 oz (75g) light muscovado raw cane sugar
1 teaspoonful vanilla essence
3 oz (75g) candied peel or raisins

1. Line the flan dish with the prepared pastry.

2. Use a wooden spoon to beat the ricotta until it is smooth, then add the cream, sugar and beaten eggs. Mix well.

3. Stir in the essence and chopped peel or raisins.

4. Fill the flan case with the mixture and cook at 350°F/180°C (Gas Mark 4) for about 45 minutes.

Note: Ricotta cheese is available from most Italian delicatessens, and has a unique, delicate taste. If, however, you cannot obtain it, cottage or curd cheese can be used instead.

HONEYED FRUIT FLAN

For Pastry
4 oz (100g) plain wholemeal flour
4 oz (100g) polyunsaturated margarine
1 tablespoonful honey
Cold water to mix

For Filling
8 oz (225g) dried apricot halves
2 large bananas
Approx. 20 firm green grapes
1 tablespoonful honey
1 tablespoonful lemon juice
1 teaspoonful cinnamon

1. Soak the apricots overnight.

2. Make the pastry by rubbing the margarine into the flour to produce a fine crumb mixture, then binding with enough water to make a firm dough.

3. Knead in the honey, then wrap in aluminium or cling foil and chill for half an hour.

4. Roll out the pastry and use to line a small flan dish; prick the bottom with a fork, then bake blind at 350°F/180°C (Gas Mark 4) for about 20 minutes, or until crisp.

5. Combine honey and lemon juice, add cinnamon, then stir in the drained plumped apricot halves, the bananas cut into chunks, and the grapes. It is important that each piece of fruit is coated in the honey syrup – you may need to make up a little more.

6. When pastry case has cooled, arrange the fruit in decorative circles. Any extra syrup can be poured over the top, and for a spicier taste, a final sprinkling of cinnamon can be added.

ALMOND FLAN

Pastry to line an 8 in. flan dish
4 tablespoonsful strawberry, raspberry or cherry jam
6 oz (175 g) light muscovado raw cane sugar
6 oz (175 g) ground almonds
3 egg whites

1. Roll out the pastry and line the flan dish carefully.

2. Spread the jam evenly across the bottom of the flan.

3. Whisk the egg whites until stiff enough to hold their own shape.

4. Combine the sugar and ground almonds; fold into the egg whites.

5. Spoon into the flan.

6. Bake at 350°F/180°C (Gas Mark 4) for 15 minutes.

TOFU FLAN

For Base
2 oz (50g) polyunsaturated margarine
4 oz (100g) rolled oats
1 oz (25g) demerara raw cane sugar

For Topping
4 oz (100g) tofu (bean curd)
2 large ripe bananas
Approx. 2 tablespoonsful maple syrup
1 lb (450g) sweetened stewed fruit (e.g. gooseberries,
    apricots, cherries, etc.)
1 teaspoonful arrowroot

1. Mix together the margarine, rolled oats and sugar, and press
   into a lightly greased flan dish. Chill.

2. Mash the drained tofu to a smooth cream with the bananas
   and maple syrup, adjusting the sweetness to suit your taste.
   Smooth over the flan base.

3. Drain the stewed fruit and bring the juice to a boil with the
   arrowroot, then cook until the sauce thickens.

4. Spoon the fruit over the tofu mixture, and top with the
   slightly cooled fruit sauce. Chill the flan before serving.

GINGER MARMALADE TART

For Pastry
6oz (175g) plain wholemeal flour
1 heaped teaspoonful ground ginger
3oz (75g) polyunsaturated margarine
1oz (25g) muscovado raw cane sugar
1 egg

For Filling
4 tablespoonsful marmalade made with raw cane sugar
4 tablespoonsful cake crumbs, preferably wholemeal
1½oz (40g) polyunsaturated margarine
1 large egg
1 tablespoonful coarsely grated orange peel – optional

1. Sift together the flour and ginger, then rub in the margarine to make a fine crumb-like mixture.

2. Stir in the sugar, then bind the dough with the beaten egg.

3. Mix well, knead lightly, adding one or two teaspoonsful water if dough is too dry. If possible, wrap in aluminium or cling foil and chill in fridge for 30 minutes.

4. Roll out pastry and line flan dish.

5. Cream together the marmalade and margarine, then add the crumbs, egg and grated peel. Mix well.

6. Spoon into the flan case and bake at 375°F/190°C (Gas Mark 5) for 20-25 minutes. Eat slightly cooled or cold.

SWEET CARROT FLAN

Pastry to line an 8 in. flan dish
1 lb (450g) carrots
2 eggs
¼ pt (150 ml) milk
1 oz (25 g) polyunsaturated margarine
2 teaspoonsful cinnamon
1 teaspoonful vanilla essence
4 oz (100 g) light muscovado raw cane sugar
2 oz (50 g) walnuts

1. Roll out the pastry and line the flan dish carefully.

2. Cook, mash and thoroughly drain the carrots, then leave to cool slightly.

3. Combine the carrots with the two beaten eggs, milk, margarine, spices, vanilla essence and sugar. Spoon into the flan case.

4. Chop the walnuts and scatter them over the carrot filling.

5. Bake at 400°F/205°C (Gas Mark 6) for 25-30 minutes, or until set.

BANANA SOUR CREAM FLAN

For Base
6 oz (175 g) wholewheat flakes
3 oz (75 g) polyunsaturated margarine
3 tablespoonsful honey

For Filling
4-5 large ripe bananas
Small carton soured cream
1-2 tablespoonsful honey
2 oz (50 g) flaked roasted almonds or coconut

1. Melt together the margarine and honey, then stir in the finely crushed wheatflakes, making sure they are well coated in the honey.

2. Grease a small flan dish, spoon in the wheatflake mixture and press firmly and evenly across the bottom and up the sides of the dish.

3. Bake at 350°F/180°C (Gas Mark 4) for 10 minutes. Leave to cool.

4. Mash the bananas as smooth as possible, then add the soured cream, and honey to taste. Pour into the flan case and sprinkle the top with flaked nuts.

5. Chill briefly before serving.

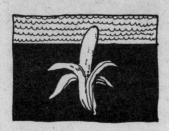

TREACLE TART

Pastry to line an 8 in. flan dish
2 oz (50g) molasses
4 oz (100g) soft wholemeal breadcrumbs
1-2 teaspoonsful lemon juice

1. Line the flan dish with the rolled out pastry, and bake it blind for 15 minutes at 400°F/205°C (Gas Mark 6).

2. In a saucepan warm the molasses and lemon juice together, then stir in the bread crumbs, making sure they are coated evenly.

3. Pour mixture into the flan case and continue baking at 350°F/180°C (Gas Mark 4) for 30 minutes more. Serve hot or cold.

CHEESE AND APPLE FLAN

Pastry to line an 8 in. flan dish
1 lb (450g) cooking or dessert apples
2-4 oz (50-100g) light muscovado raw cane sugar
1 teaspoonful cinnamon
¼ teaspoonful nutmeg
¼ teaspoonful allspice
4 oz (100g) Cheddar cheese
1 oz (25g) plain wholemeal flour
1 oz (25g) polyunsaturated margarine

1. Line the flan dish with the rolled out pastry.

2. Peel and core the apples, then slice thinly.

3. Mix together the spices and flour; add the grated cheese and raw cane sugar, (if using cooking apples you will need 4 oz (100g), but with dessert apples 2 oz (50g), will probably be sufficient).

4. Stir in the slices of apple.

5. Put this mixture into the pastry case and scatter with small knobs of margarine.

6. Bake at 400°F/205°C (Gas Mark 6) for 30-40 minutes, or until the crust is golden brown.

PECAN PIE

Pastry to line an 8 in. flan dish
8 oz (225 g) molasses raw cane sugar
8 oz (225 g) honey or syrup
2 oz (50 g) polyunsaturated margarine
3 eggs
5 oz (150 g) halved pecan nuts

1. Carefully line the flan dish with the pastry and set aside.

2. Mix together the sugar, honey and melted margarine.

3. Beat the eggs, then add to the sugar mixture, and combine thoroughly.

4. Stir in the pecans.

5. Pour the filling into the flan dish and bake at 400°F/200°C (Gas Mark 6) for 10 minutes, then at 350°F/180°C (Gas Mark 4) for about 30 minutes more, or until the filling has set.

6. Serve warm (not hot) or let cool completely.

Note: Walnuts can be used in place of the pecans, if desired.

GOOSEBERRY FOOL FLAN

Pastry to line an 8 in. flan dish
1 lb (450 g) fresh or frozen gooseberries
3 oz (75 g) demerara raw cane sugar
1 teaspoonful vanilla essence
½ pt (275 ml) whipping cream (or ¼ pt single, ¼ pt double cream)
Roasted flaked almonds – optional

1. Line a flan dish with the pastry, and bake blind at 375°F/190°C (Gas Mark 5) for 20-30 minutes, or until crisp and golden. Set aside to get completely cold.

2. Clean, top and tail the gooseberries, then cook in a covered pan with the sugar and the minimum amount of water until soft.

3. Drain the gooseberries, then sieve them to make a *purée*.

4. In a separate bowl whip the cream until thick; combine this with the gooseberry *purée*.

5. Spoon the mixture into the prepared flan case, smooth the top, and leave in the refrigerator (or somewhere cool) until required. Scatter with nuts before serving.

Note: Any fruits can be used in this recipe, including dried fruits – apricots are particularly delicious with grated lemon or orange peel.

QUARK TORTE
(Cottage Cheese Flan)

Pastry to line an 8 in. flan dish
8 oz (225 g) *Quark*
Approx. 4 tablespoonsful cream or creamy milk
4 oz (100 g) light muscovado raw cane sugar
2 eggs, separated
1 tablespoonful grated lemon peel or candied peel
1 teaspoonful cinnamon
2 oz (50 g) currants

1. Line the flan case with the pastry; bake blind at 400°F/205°C (Gas Mark 6) for 10 minutes.

2. Strain the *Quark* until dry and crumbly, then use a fork to blend it with the cream.

3. Add the sugar, egg yolks, peel, currants and cinnamon. Mix until thoroughly combined.

4. Beat the egg whites until stiff, then fold them into the *Quark* mixture.

5. Spoon into the flan case and bake at 350°F/180°C (Gas Mark 4) for 40-50 minutes, or until set. Serve warm or cold.

Note: Quark is a continental version of cottage cheese. It is available in this country, but if you cannot find it, you will get similar results with cottage cheese.

UPSIDE-DOWN APPLE CRUMBLE

For Base
8 oz (225g) plain wholemeal flour
4 oz (100g) polyunsaturated margarine
1-2 teaspoonsful mixed spice

For Filling
8 oz (225g) dessert apples
2 oz (50g) raisins and/or sultanas
2 oz (50g) roasted peanuts
2 tablespoonsful tahini (sesame spread)
1-2 teaspoonsful honey

1. Sift the flour into a bowl, and use fingertips to work in the margarine so that you get a crumb-like mixture. Add spices.

2. Lightly grease an 8 in. flan dish (or, better still, a loose-bottomed flan tin) and press most of the crumb mixture evenly and firmly across the base and up the sides.

3. Bake at 400°F/205°C (Gas Mark 6) for 10 minutes, then cool slightly.

4. Core and slice the apples as finely as possible; mix with the dried fruit and coarsely chopped peanuts.

5. Combine the tahini and honey, and stir the sauce into the fruit and nut mixture to give an even coating.

6. Spoon into the flan case and sprinkle with the extra crumble mix; bake at 375°F/190°C (Gas Mark 5) for 20 minutes. Serve hot or cold.

YOGURT CUSTARD FLAN

For Base
4 oz (100g) muesli
2 oz (50g) polyunsaturated margarine

For Topping
2 eggs
½ pt (275 ml) plain yogurt
1 oz (25g) light muscovado raw cane sugar
1 teaspoonful almond essence
¼ pt (150 ml) milk
1 oz (25g) roasted flaked almonds

1. Melt the margarine; stir in the muesli; press the mixture firmly and evenly into a lightly greased flan dish.

2. Beat together the eggs and sugar, then add the yogurt and almond extract, and continue mixing until smooth.

3. Stir in the milk.

4. Pour the custard onto the base and sprinkle the top with flaked almonds, then put, at once, into the oven.

5. Bake at 250°F/140°C (Gas Mark 1) for about 30 minutes, or until a knife inserted in the custard comes out clean.

6. Serve hot or cold; on its own or with fresh, stewed or dried fruit.

Note: Vary the flavour of this flan by using vanilla essence instead of almond, and topping it with ground nutmeg instead of nuts. Or omit the essences and add instead one tablespoonful of carob powder for a chocolate-flavoured custard.

FRANZIPAN FLAN

Pastry to line an 8 in. flan dish
½ pt (275 ml) milk
3 oz (75 g) wholewheat semolina
4 oz (100 g) polyunsaturated margarine
4 oz (100 g) light muscovado raw cane sugar
1 egg
2 oz (50 g) *glacé* cherries
2 oz (50 g) raisins
4 oz (100 g) raw cane sugar marzipan

1. Roll out the pastry, line the flan dish and set aside.

2. In a saucepan, cook together the semolina and milk until the mixture thickens.

3. In a bowl, and using a wooden spoon, cream together the margarine and sugar, add the egg and then the slightly cooled semolina.

4. Roughly chop the cherries and marzipan and stir them into the mixture with the raisins.

5. Spread evenly in the flan case and bake at 400°F/205°C (Gas Mark 6) for 20 minutes, then reduce heat to 350°F/180°C (Gas Mark 4) and cook for a further 20 minutes until the filling is set. Serve cold.

Note: This is based on a traditional recipe, but as *glacé* cherries tend to be full of preservatives, you may wish to replace them with grated lemon peel, or raw cane sugar candied peel. Chopped dried apricots also go well with the other ingredients.

STRAWBERRY CHEESECAKE

For Base
8 oz (225 g) digestive biscuits
4 oz (100 g) polyunsaturated margarine

For Filling
8 oz (225 g) cream or curd cheese
$^1/_3$ pt (180 ml) milk
2 oz (50 g) light muscovado raw cane sugar
1 teaspoonful lemon juice

For Topping
8 oz (225 g) fresh strawberries
1 tablespoonful honey
2 tablespoonsful water
1 teaspoonful arrowroot

1. Melt the margarine, stir in the crushed biscuits, and use the mixture to line the base of a small flan dish. Leave in cool place to set firm.

2. With a wooden spoon, beat together the cream cheese and milk, add the lemon juice and sugar. Mix thoroughly. Pour into the flan case and refrigerate for at least a few hours, preferably longer.

3. Shortly before serving the cheesecake, arrange the halved strawberries decoratively on the top. Make a syrup by combining the honey, water and arrowroot in a saucepan, and bringing to the boil. Cool slightly, spoon carefully over the fruit, and return to the refrigerator until needed.

Note: Any other fruit can be used as a topping for this cheesecake, either fresh or stewed. In an emergency, try it with pineapple tinned in natural juices, and use the juice with arrowroot to make the sauce.

DRIED FRUIT FLAN

Pastry to line an 8 in. flan dish
4 oz (100g) dried prunes
4 oz (100g) dried apricots
4 oz (100g) dried apple rings
4 oz (100g) raisins
2 oz (50g) demerara raw cane sugar – optional
1 tablespoonful grated lemon or orange peel
1 teaspoonful vanilla essence (or orange juice with orange rind)
2 oz (50g) walnut pieces
2 oz (50g) polyunsaturated margarine

1. Line the flan dish with the prepared pastry and set aside in the cool while you prepare the filling.

2. Cook the prunes, apricots and apple rings in the minimum of water until just soft (if they have been soaked first, this only takes a few minutes). Drain, then dab dry with a paper towel.

3. Remove the stones from the prunes, and cut all the fruit into chunks.

4. In a bowl stir together the fruit (including the raisins), sugar, grated peel, essence or juice, and chopped walnut pieces.

5. Melt the margarine and stir into the other ingredients, mixing well before spooning the mixture into the flan case.

6. Bake at 350°F/180°C (Gas Mark 4) for about 45 minutes, or until the pastry is crisp. Serve slightly cooled.

LEMON MERINGUE PIE

Pastry to line an 8 in. flan dish

For Lemon Filling
6 oz (175 g) light muscovado raw cane sugar
2 oz (50 g) plain wholemeal flour, with bran sifted out
½ pt (275 ml) water
1 oz (25 g) polyunsaturated margarine
2 egg yolks
2 medium lemons

For Meringue
2 egg whites
4 oz (100 g) light muscovado raw cane sugar

1. Line a flan dish with the pastry, prick the bottom, and bake blind at 400°F/205°C (Gas Mark 6) for 15 minutes.

2. Meanwhile, combine the sugar, flour and water in a saucepan, and bring gently to the boil, stirring continually.

3. Remove from heat and cool for a few minutes before beating in the margarine and two egg yolks. Add the juice and grated rind of the lemons.

4. Pour slightly cooled lemon filling into the prepared case.

5. Make the meringue by whisking the two egg whites until stiff enough to stand in peaks, beat in half of the sugar, then fold in the rest.

6. Pile the meringue on top of the filling, making sure it is covered completely, then use a fork to make a decorative pattern.

7. Bake at 300°F/150°C (Gas Mark 2) for 30 minutes, or until meringue is crisp and beginning to brown. Serve cool or cold.

FRUIT IN NUT CASE

For Base
Pastry to line an 8 in. flan dish
4 oz (100 g) Brazil nuts, ground finely
2 oz (50 g) demerara raw cane sugar – optional

For Filling
1 lb (450 g) greengages
8 oz (225 g) red plums
4 oz (100 g) demerara raw cane sugar
1 tablespoonful lemon juice

1. Add the nuts and sugar to the pastry before rolling out and using to line an 8-9 in. flan dish. (Any extra pastry can be used to make a decorative lattice on top.)

2. Bake blind at 375°F/190°C (Gas Mark 5) for 10 minutes, then remove from oven and cool.

3. Meanwhile, simmer the washed, stoned fruit with the minimum of water in two separate pans, sharing the lemon juice and most of the sugar between them. Remove when fruit is soft, but still holds shape.

4. Strain excess liquid from fruits, mix gently together, and pile into prepared flan case; sprinkle top with a little more sugar.

5. Serve warm or chilled.

6. Any extra juice can be brought to the boil with a teaspoonful of arrowroot to make a sauce.

RAISIN BUTTERMILK PIE

Pastry to line an 8 in. flan dish
3 oz (75 g) polyunsaturated margarine
6 oz (175 g) honey
1 oz (25 g) plain wholemeal flour
½ pt (275 ml) buttermilk
4 oz (100 g) raisins
2 teaspoonsful mixed spice
2 large eggs

1. Roll out the pastry and use to line a flan dish.

2. Cream together the margarine, honey and egg yolks, combining them thoroughly.

3. Sift together the flour and spice, then add to the first mixture.

4. Beat in the buttermilk and raisins.

5. Whisk the egg whites until stiff. Fold carefully into the mixture.

6. Spoon into the flan crust and smooth the top. Bake at 325°F/165°C (Gas Mark 3) for 40-50 minutes, or until set.

RHUBARB AND CUSTARD TART

Pastry to line an 8 in. flan dish
1 lb (450g) rhubarb
2 tablespoonsful honey
1-2 teaspoonsful mixed spices
2 eggs
½ pt (275 ml) milk
2 oz (50g) light muscovado raw cane sugar

1. Roll out the pastry, line a flan dish, and bake blind at 400°F/205°C (Gas Mark 6) for 15 minutes. Leave to cool slightly.

2. Using the minimum of water, simmer the chopped rhubarb with the honey and mixed spices. Remove from the heat when the fruit is cooked, but still retains its shape. Drain well.

3. Beat together the eggs and sugar.

4. Heat the milk gently until hot but not boiling, then pour over the egg mixture, stirring continuously.

5. Continue cooking very gently, still stirring, until the mixture begins to thicken, then leave to cool slightly.

6. Arrange the rhubarb over the base of the flan, then carefully pour in the custard. Smooth the top.

7. Bake at 300°F/150°C (Gas Mark 2) for 20-30 minutes, or until the custard is set firm.

NUT TORTE

Pastry to line an 8 in. flan dish
8 oz (225 g) demerara raw cane sugar
1 oz (25 g) plain wholemeal flour
6 eggs, separated
12 oz (350 g) hazel or walnuts
1 teaspoonful grated lemon peel
1 tablespoonful orange or lemon juice
1 tablespoonful demerara raw cane sugar

1. Line the flan dish with the rolled out pastry.

2. Beat together the sugar and egg yolks.

3. Grind the nuts, add them to the sugar and egg mixture, and mix well.

4. Whip the egg whites until stiff, then fold them into the mixture, a spoonful at a time, alternating with a sprinkling of the flour.

5. Add the finely grated peel and the juice.

6. Pour or spoon into the prepared flan case and bake at 350°F/180°C (Gas Mark 4) for 40 to 50 minutes.

7. Take from oven and sprinkle with sugar. Serve cold.

CRUNCHY PEAR FLAN

For Base
6 oz (175 g) crunchy oat cereal
2 oz (50 g) plain wholemeal flour
2 oz (50 g) polyunsaturated margarine

For Topping
1 lb (450 g) pears
2-4 oz (50-100 g) demerara raw cane sugar
1 teaspoonful spice
2 oz (50 g) raisins
2 oz (50 g) crunchy oat cereal

1. Combine the flour and wholewheat cereal; melt the margarine and blend with the cereal.

2. Press the mixture firmly and evenly into a lightly greased 8 in. or 9 in. flan dish. Cook blind for about 15-20 minutes at 375°F/190°C (Gas Mark 5), or until crisp. Leave to cool.

3. Peel, core and slice the pears, then put them into a saucepan and add the sugar, spice, and just enough water to cover them.

4. Simmer until tender, then remove from heat, stir in the raisins, and set aside for 10 minutes.

5. Spoon fruit into the flan case as evenly as possible, and sprinkle with the oat cereal. Serve any left-over syrup in a separate jug.

SWEET RICE FLAN

Pastry to line an 8 in. flan dish
6 oz (175 g) cooked brown rice
4 oz (100 g) honey
1 egg
8 oz (225 g) dessert apples
4 oz (100 g) currants
1-2 teaspoonsful mixed spice
Plain yogurt to serve

1. Line flan dish with prepared pastry and cook blind at 400°F/205°C (Gas Mark 6) for 10 minutes. Set aside.

2. Drain rice well, then put into a bowl, and mix in the honey, beaten egg, spices, raisins and peeled, chopped apples.

3. Spread the mixture in the flan base, and return it to the oven. Cook for 20-30 minutes at 350°F/180°C (Gas Mark 4). Chill, then serve with yogurt.

FROZEN LEMON PIE

Pastry to line an 8 in. flan dish
8 oz (225 g) cream cheese
1 small carton plain yogurt
4-6 tablespoonsful lemon curd made with raw cane sugar

1. Line the flan dish with the pastry, and bake blind at 375°F/190°C (Gas Mark 5) for 20-30 minutes, or until crisp and golden. Set aside to get completely cold.

2. Beat the cream cheese until smooth, then mix well with the yogurt (first pouring off any excess liquid).

3. Add the lemon curd to taste, and blend well.

4. Spoon the mixture into the cold flan case, smooth the top, and chill in the freezer for at least 2 hours.

5. Serve straight from the freezer.

MAPLE CRUNCH FLAN

Pastry to line an 8 in. flan dish
3 tablespoonsful maple syrup
1 tablespoonful lemon juice
2 medium bananas
2 oz (50 g) wholewheat flakes

1. Roll out the prepared pastry and use to line the flan dish.

2. In a saucepan, gently heat the maple syrup with the lemon juice, then stir in the crushed wheatflakes.

3. Either mash the peeled bananas, and stir them into the syrup-wheatflakes mixture and top with wheatflakes, or slice and layer them across the base of the flan.

4. Pour the mixture into the flan, spreading as evenly as possible.

5. Bake at 400°F/200°C (Gas Mark 6) for 30 minutes. Serve hot with custard or cold with yogurt or cream.

CHOCOLATE CREAM FLAN

Pastry to line an 8 in. flan dish
4 oz (100g) plain raw sugar chocolate
4 eggs
¼ pt (150ml) whipping cream

1. Roll out the pastry, line a flan dish, and bake blind at 375°F/190°C (Gas Mark 5) for 20-30 minutes, or until cooked. Set aside to cool.

2. Grate or finely chop the chocolate, melt it in a bowl over a pan of hot water, then remove from the heat and whisk in the egg yolks.

3. Cool the creamy mixture; beat the egg whites until stiff and fold into the chocolate.

4. Spoon the mixture into the cold cooked flan case, even the surface, and decorate with whipped cream. A little extra grated chocolate and flaked almonds can also be used.

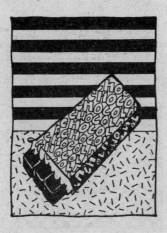

APRICOT GINGER PIE

For Base
8 oz (225 g) wholemeal ginger biscuits
3 oz (75 g) polyunsaturated margarine

For Filling
1 lb (450 g) dried or fresh apricots
1-2 oz (25-50 g) light muscovado raw cane sugar
¼ pt (150 ml) whipping cream
Squeeze of lemon juice
1 egg white

1. Crush the biscuits as finely as possible and melt the margarine; combine thoroughly; press the mixture against the base and sides of the flan dish.

2. Simmer the apricots with the sugar and just a little water until soft enough to *purée* by pressing through a sieve, or putting into a blender. Add the juice.

3. Whip the cream lightly and fold into the apricot *purée*, then add the stiffly whisked egg white.

4. Spoon the mixture into the flan case and chill before serving. This may be sprinkled with some walnut pieces, crunchy oat cereal, or more crumbled ginger biscuits. Chopped preserved ginger can also be added.

MINCEMEAT FLAN DE LUXE

Pastry to line an 8 in. flan dish
8 oz (225 g) raw sugar mincemeat
2 oz (50 g) desiccated coconut
2 oz (50 g) cherries – optional
1 tablespoonful brandy – optional

1. Use most of the pastry to line a flan dish, then bake blind for 15 minutes at 375°F/190°C (Gas Mark 5).

2. Mix together the mincemeat, coconut and brandy. (If you prefer, you can use a little orange juice to moisten the mixture). Stir in the chopped *glacé* cherries, if liked.

3. Spoon the mixture into the flan case and make a lattice decoration with the extra pastry; bake at the same temperature as before for a further 15 minutes, or until the pastry is cooked. Serve warm or cold.

FRENCH APPLE FLAN

Fleur pastry to line a 7 in. flan dish
Approx. 1lb (450g) cooking apples
2oz (50g) light muscovado raw cane sugar
Squeeze of lemon juice
4oz (100g) raw sugar apricot jam

1. Line a flan dish with the pastry and bake blind at 400°F/200°C (Gas Mark 6) for 10 minutes.

2. Carefully peel, core and quarter the apples, putting them in cold water and lemon juice so that they stay white.

3. Simmer about a third of the apples with the sugar and a little water to make a *purée*; spread over the base of the flan.

4. Cut the remaining apples into thin slices and arrange attractively in circles over the *purée*, making sure it is completely covered.

5. Sieve the apricot jam and warm, then brush it over the apples; bake the flan at 375°F/190°C (Gas Mark 5) for 20-25 minutes, or until the pastry is cooked and apples tender. Serve warm or cold.

COCONUT DATE PIE

Pastry to line an 8 in. flan dish
3 eggs
¼ pt (140 ml) single cream or top of milk
4 tablespoonsful honey
1 oz (25 g) wholemeal bread or cake crumbs
1-2 teaspoonsful mixed spice
4 oz (100 g) dates
3 oz (75 g) desiccated coconut

1. Roll out the pastry; line the flan dish carefully and set aside.

2. Beat the eggs, then add the cream, honey and spice, stirring well.

3. Chop the dates into small pieces and add to the mixture with the fine crumbs and most of the coconut.

4. Spoon into the flan case and smooth the top; bake at 425°F/220°C (Gas Mark 7) for 15 minutes.

5. Sprinkle the remaining desiccated coconut over the flan, lower oven temperature to 325°F/170°C (Gas Mark 3), and bake for 20-25 minutes more, or until the pie is firm in the centre. Serve cold.

PENNSYLVANIA DUTCH SHOO FLY PIE

Pastry to line an 8 in. flan dish
2 oz (50 g) polyunsaturated margarine
3 oz (75 g) plain wholemeal flour
3 oz (75 g) light muscovado raw cane sugar
4 oz (100 g) honey
4 oz (100 g) molasses
1 egg
¼ pt (140 ml) boiling water
Bare teaspoonful bicarbonate of soda

1. Line the flan dish with the rolled out pastry.

2. Make a crumb-like mixture by rubbing the margarine into the flour, then add the sugar.

3. Dissolve the soda in the boiling water; add the molasses and honey and stir until thoroughly blended. Allow to cool.

4. Add the beaten egg to the molasses and honey mixture before pouring it into the uncooked flan case; sprinkle the crumb mixture over the top.

5. Bake for 10 minutes at 400°F/200°C (Gas Mark 6), then for 25-30 minutes more at 350°F/180°C (Gas Mark 4), or until the filling is set. Leave to cool.

FRESH FRUIT TARTS

8 oz (225 g) shortcrust pastry
Small bunch black grapes
Small bunch white grapes
1 large fresh peach or orange
Small bunch blackcurrants
A few raspberries or redcurrants
Small firm banana
¼ pt (140 ml) fresh orange or other fruit juice
1 teaspoonful arrowroot

1. Roll out the pastry and use it to line individual patty tins (preferably not too small or there won't be enough room for a decorative fruit arrangement).

2. Bake the tarts blind at 375°F/190°C (Gas Mark 5) for about 10 minutes, or until cooked. Set aside to cool.

3. Wash and dry the fruit; peel and slice the peach and banana.

4. Divide the fruit between the tart shells, arranging it to look attractive and colourful.

5. In a saucepan blend the arrowroot with the fruit juice; bring to the boil; stir until smooth and thick.

6. Cool the glaze for a few minutes, then brush it over the fruit. Leave to cool completely before serving the tarts.

Note: You can use an equal amount of pastry and filling to make one large flan if you prefer, but small tarts look especially enticing, especially when being served to children. Use whatever combination of fruit you like, just make sure you include as many colours as possible.

ICE CREAM FLAN

For Sponge Base
2 eggs
2 oz (50g) raw cane sugar, preferably powdered in a grinder
2 oz (50g) plain wholemeal flour

For Filling
8 oz (225g) fresh raspberries
Vanilla ice cream, preferably home-made
3 tablespoonsful raw sugar raspberry jam
A little water

1. In a basin, whisk together the eggs and sugar until thick.

2. Fold in the sieved flour gently.

3. Line a flan case with silver foil, and spread the sponge mixture into it evenly; bake for 20 minutes at 400°F/200°C (Gas Mark 6); leave to cool before peeling off foil.

4. Shortly before serving the flan, arrange the washed and dried fruit across the base of the sponge, and top with rounded spoonsful of the ice cream.

5. Heat the jam with a little water, stirring continually, to make a sauce; trickle decoratively over the ice cream and serve.

Note: Any fruit can be used in this flan, or serve it just with ice cream, honey sauce and chopped nuts. Although it should be served almost straight away, it will taste better if the ice cream has been allowed to soften a little before being put into the flan.

PINEAPPLE HONEY FLAN

Pastry to line an 8 in. flan dish
1 small pineapple or 1 large tin pineapple slices in natural
  juice
3 oz (75 g) raisins
2 tablespoonsful honey
1 tablespoonful lemon juice
1-2 teaspoonsful grated lemon rind

1. Roll out the pastry and line a flan dish; bake blind at
    375°F/190°C (Gas Mark 5) for 20 minutes.

2. If using fresh pineapple, peel carefully and slice into thin
    rings; if using tinned, drain off the juice.

3. Arrange the rings attractively in the flan base and sprinkle
    with raisins.

4. Mix together the lemon juice, rind and honey, and pour
    over the fruit. (You can use the pineapple juice instead, if
    you wish, but the lemon gives a better flavour.)

5. Return to the oven, lower the temperature to 350°F/180°C
    (Gas Mark 4) and cook for ten minutes, or until the crust is
    crisp. Serve warm or cold.

AVOCADO LEMON FLAN

For Base
8 oz (225 g) digestive biscuits
4 oz (100 g) polyunsaturated margarine
2 tablespoonsful honey – optional

For Filling
1 large ripe avocado
1 packet lemon-flavoured agar-agar
¼ pt (150 ml) whipping cream or double cream
Extra cream to serve – optional

1. Make the crunchy base by melting the margarine and stirring in the well crushed biscuits; add the honey if liked.

2. Press the mixture into a small flan dish – lining it with silver foil first helps make it easier to remove when chilled.

3. Set aside somewhere cool to firm up.

4. mash the avocado to a *purée*; whip the cream lightly and add this to the avocado.

5. Make up the jelly with barely ¾ pt (420 ml) of water and, when slightly cooled, mix well with the avocado and cream.

6. Leave to begin to set, then whisk again before piling the filling into the flan case and chilling. Serve decorated with more cream on special occasions.

FRUIT CRUMBLE IN A FLAN

Pastry to line an 8in. flan dish
1lb (450g) cooking apples
8oz (225g) blackberries
2oz (50g) raw cane sugar
Squeeze of lemon juice

For Topping
1oz (25g) polyunsaturated margarine
2oz (50g) plain wholemeal flour
2oz (50g) raw cane sugar
1-2 teaspoonsful ground coriander

1. Prepare the pastry, roll it out, and line the flan dish.

2. Peel, core and finely slice the apples; mix well with the
    washed and drained blackberries, sugar and lemon juice.

3. Pile the fruit into the flan case and smooth the top.

4. Make a crumble topping: rub the margarine into the flour
    with your fingertips to make a crumb-like mixture, then stir
    in the sugar and coriander.

5. Sprinkle the crumble topping evenly over the fruit and bake
    the flan at 350°F/180°C (Gas Mark 4) for 30-45 minutes, or
    until the pastry and fruit are cooked. Serve hot or cold when
    it is especially good with yogurt.

PEACH AND HAZELNUT FLAN

For Base
Pastry to line an 8in. flan dish
1oz (25g) roasted hazelnuts, coarsely ground

For Filling
4 small ripe peaches
4 tablespoonsful raw sugar apricot jam
Squeeze of lemon juice
1oz (25g) roasted hazelnuts

1. When making up the pastry, blend in the ground nuts, then roll out and line a flan dish in the usual way; bake blind at 400°F/200°C (Gas Mark 6) for 20 minutes, or until cooked.

2. In a small pan, heat the apricot jam, lemon juice and a few spoonsful of water to make a sauce; leave to cool slightly.

3. Halve and stone the peaches, then arrange cut-side down in the cooled flan case; distribute the sauce evenly over the fruit; top with the chopped hazelnuts.

4. Chill briefly if not needed immediately, but do not make up this flan too long before you intend to serve it as it is best when fresh.

PINEAPPLE FLAN WITH TOFU

Pastry to line a 6in. flan dish
12oz (350g) tofu
1 small pineapple or tinned equivalent (preferably tinned
    in natural juice)
Honey to taste – optional
Cinnamon

1. Make up the pastry and bake it blind at 400°F/200°C (Gas
    Mark 6) for 20 minutes, or until crisp.

2. Drain the excess liquid from the tofu, cut into small cubes,
    and put into a blender with the drained, cubed pineapple;
    blend until completely smooth.

3. If you like a sweeter taste add a little honey; if the mixture is
    very thick, add some of the pineapple juice.

4. Spoon evenly into the cooled flan case and chill well before
    serving sprinkled with the cinnamon. (A more decorative
    topping can be made by crushing a little of the pineapple
    with the spice and scattering it over the flan.)

Note: Although this flan can be made without a blender, the
filling must be very well mashed to get the smooth texture that
makes it so delicious.

INDEX

INDEX